FOR ORGANS, PIANOS & ELECTRONIC KEYBOARDS

E-Z PLAY TODAY

147

Great Instrumentals

ISBN 978-1-4950-2612-6

HAL•LEONARD®
CORPORATION
7777 W. BLUEMOUND RD. P.O. BOX 13819 MILWAUKEE, WI 53213

E-Z Play® Today Music Notation © 1975 by HAL LEONARD CORPORATION
E-Z PLAY and EASY ELECTRONIC KEYBOARD MUSIC are registered trademarks of HAL LEONARD CORPORATION.

Visit Hal Leonard Online at
www.halleonard.com

4 ALLEY CAT

6 BATMAN THEME

10 BEATNIK FLY

18 CISSY STRUT

13 CLASSICAL GAS

20 FEELS SO GOOD

26 GREEN ONIONS

30 THE HAPPY ORGAN

34 HAWAII FIVE-O THEME

36 HONKY TONK (PARTS 1 & 2)

23 LAST DATE

40 LOVE IS BLUE (L'AMOUR EST BLEU)

42 MIDNIGHT IN MOSCOW

45 MISIRLOU

48 MISSION: IMPOSSIBLE THEME

52 PETER GUNN

56 THE PINK PANTHER

58 PIPELINE

64 REBEL 'ROUSER

66 SLEEPWALK

68 STRANGER ON THE SHORE

70 THE STRIPPER

61 TEQUILA

72 WALK DON'T RUN

75 WIPE OUT

78 Registration Guide

Alley Cat

Registration 8
Rhythm: Ragtime

By Frank Bjorn

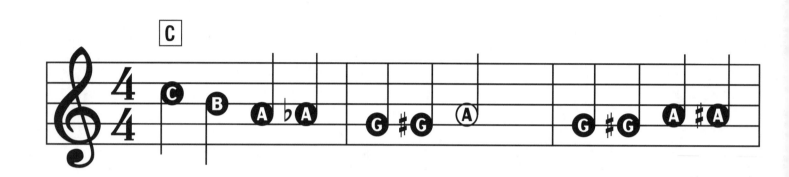

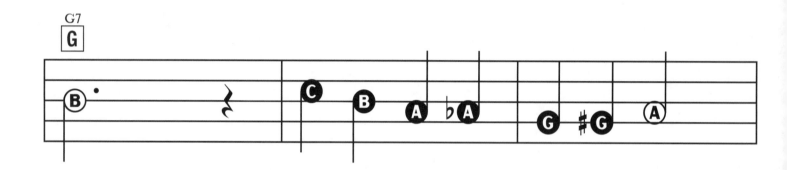

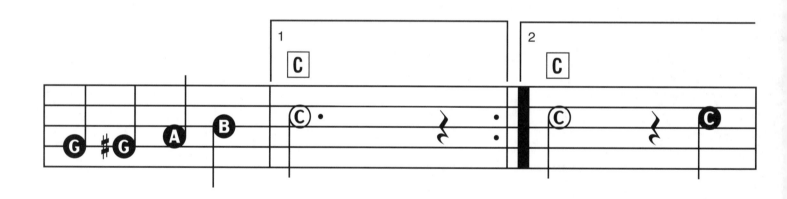

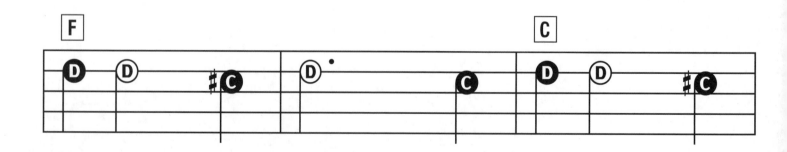

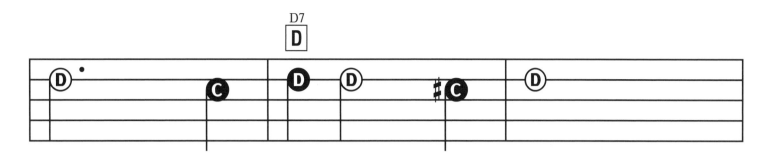

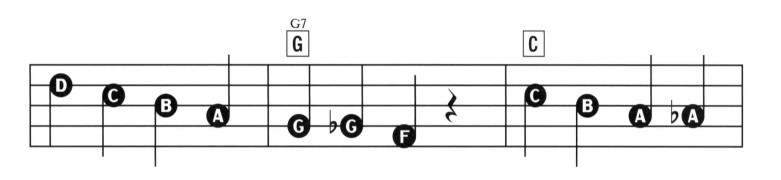

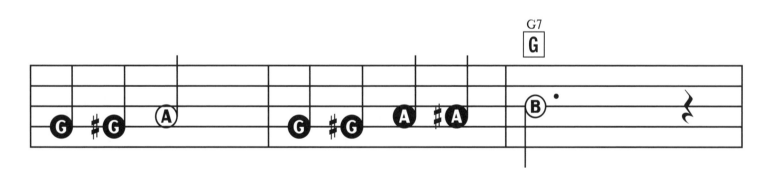

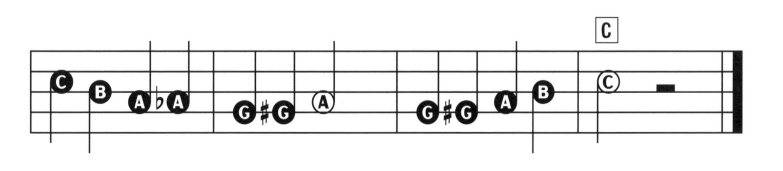

Batman Theme
Theme from the TV Series

Registration 7
Rhythm: Rock

Words and Music by
Neal Hefti

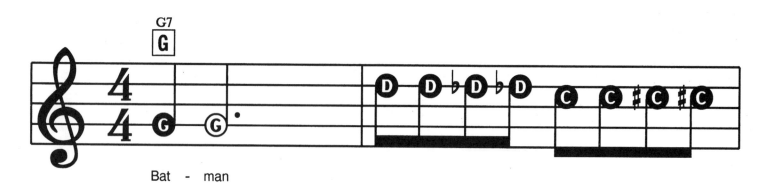

Bat - man

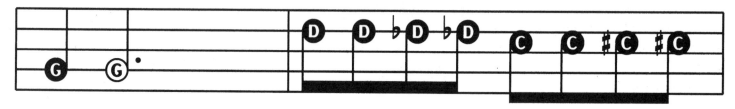

Bat - man

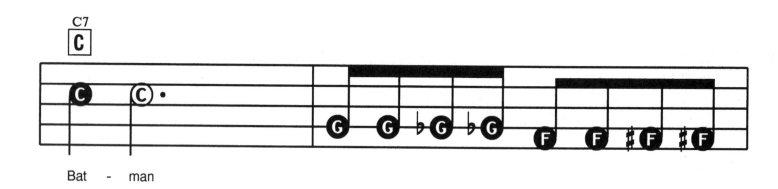

Bat - man

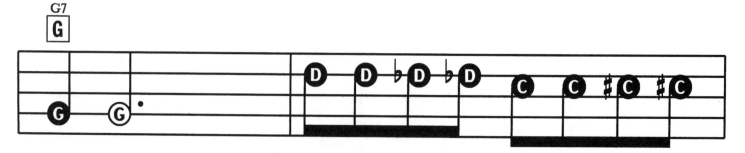

Bat - man

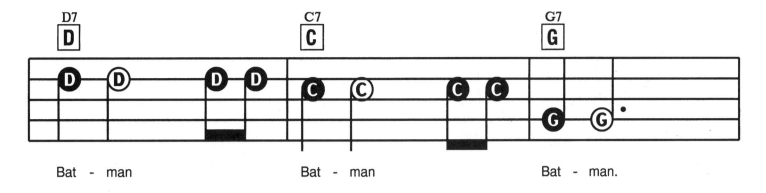

Bat - man   Bat - man   Bat - man.

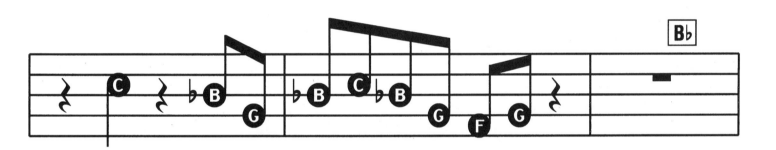

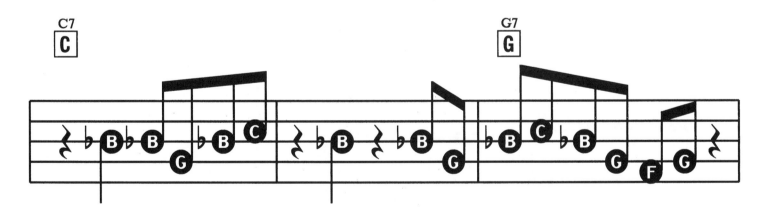

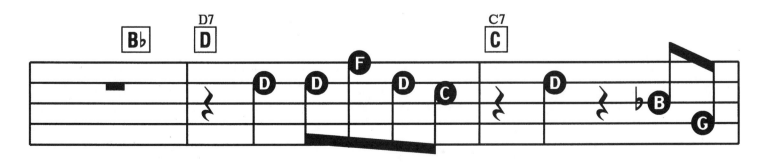

8

Bat - man

Bat - man

Bat - man

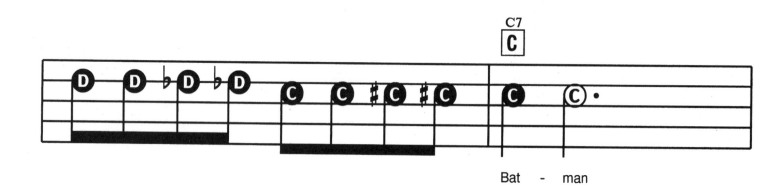

Bat - man

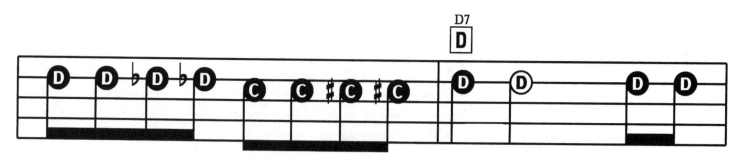

Bat - man

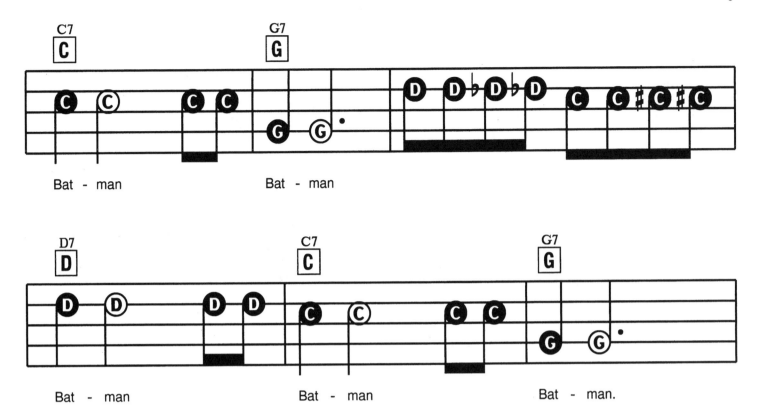

Bat - man   Bat - man

Bat - man   Bat - man   Bat - man.

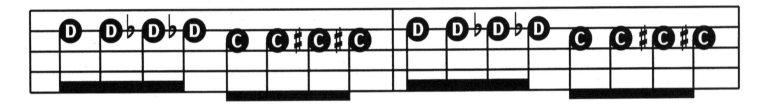

Dah - dah - dah - dah - dah - dah - dah - dah - dah - dah - dah - dah - dah - dah - dah - dah -

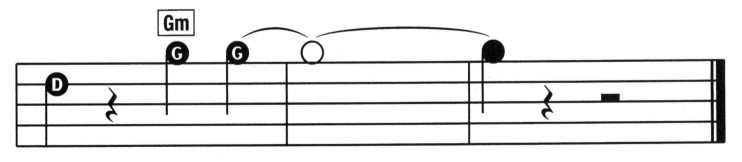

dah   Bat - man. _____

Beatnik Fly

Registration 4
Rhythm: Rock

Words and Music by Ira Mack
and Tom King

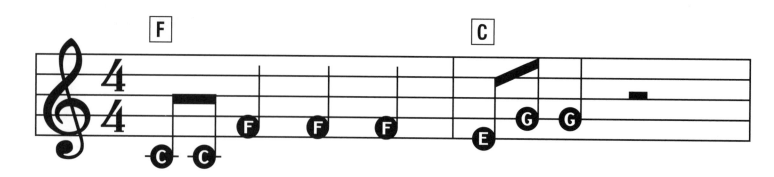

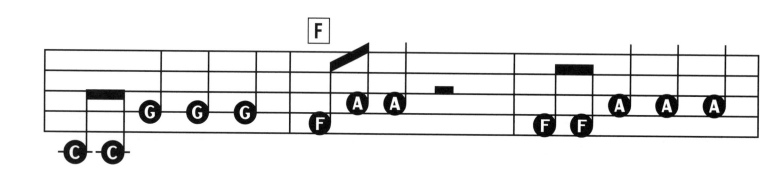

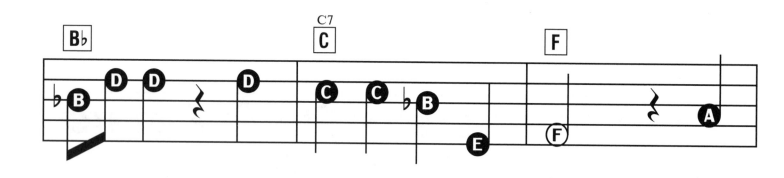

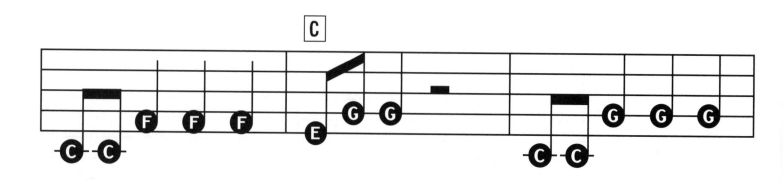

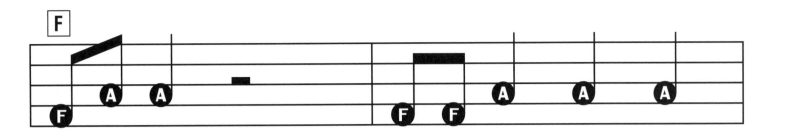

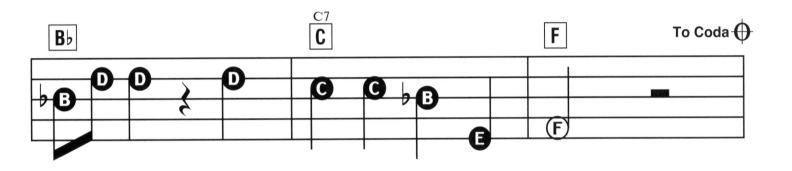

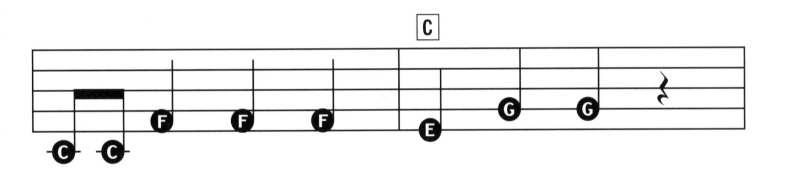

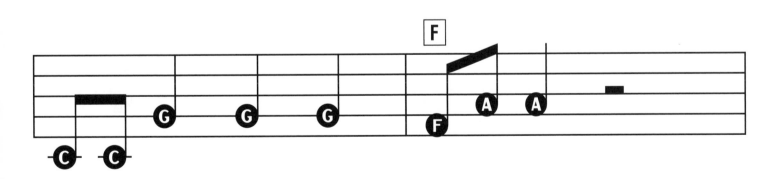

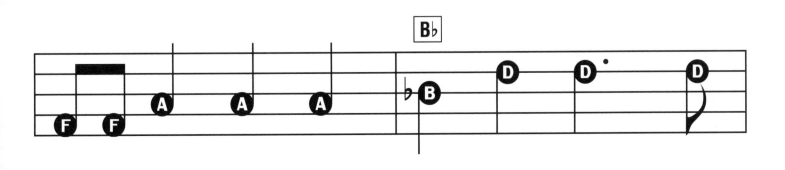

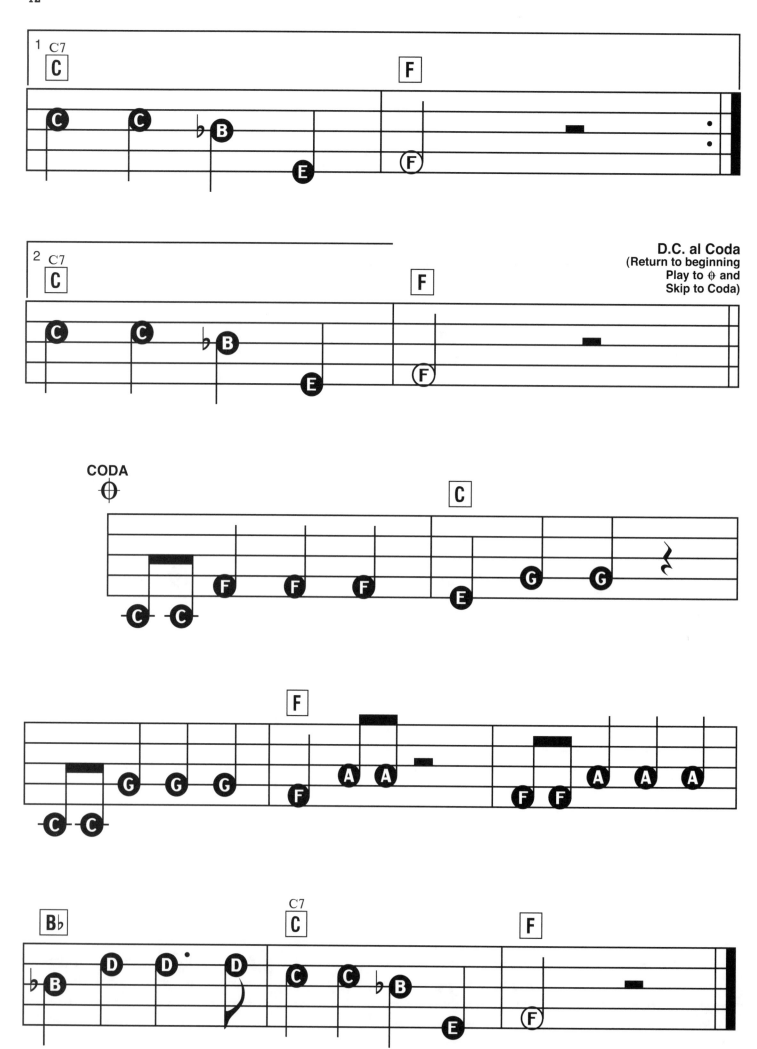

Classical Gas

Registration 4
Rhythm: Latin

Music by Mason Williams

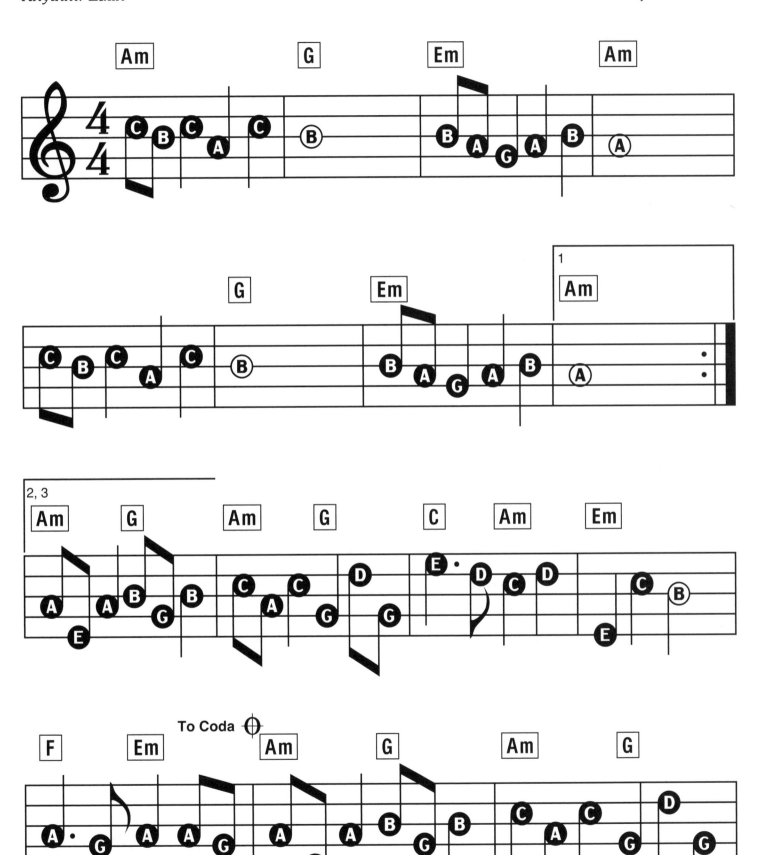

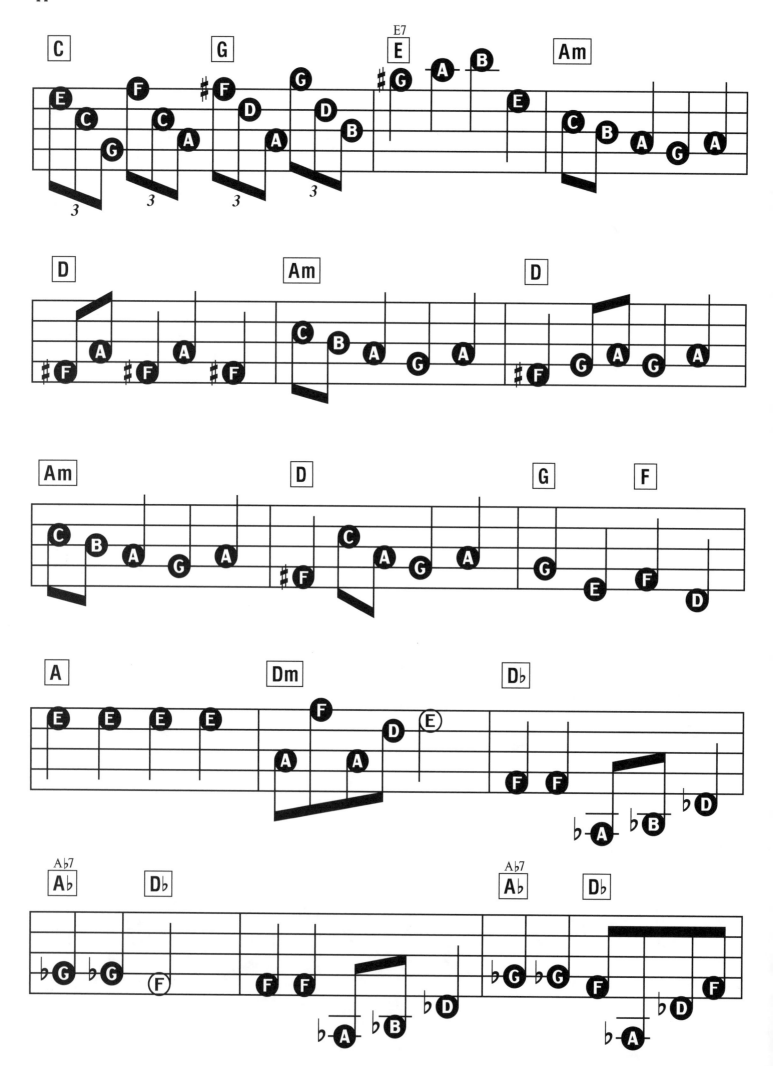

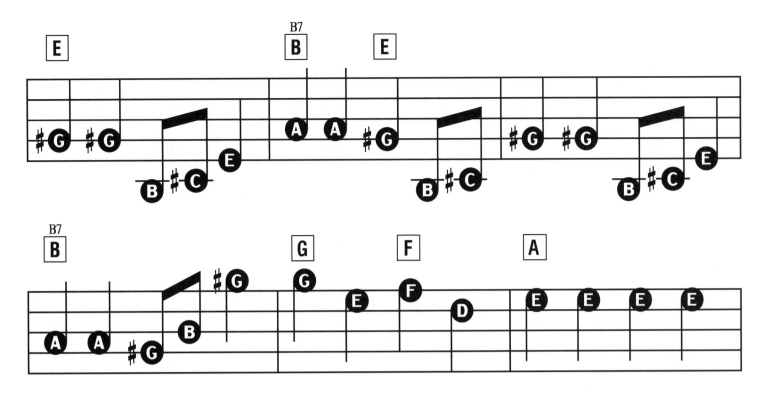

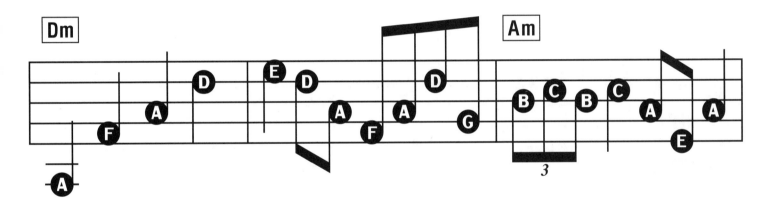

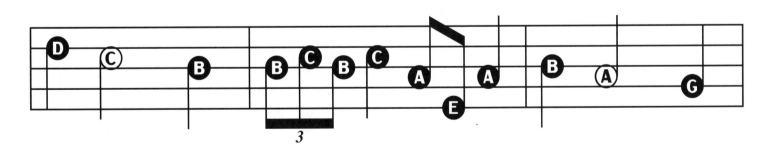

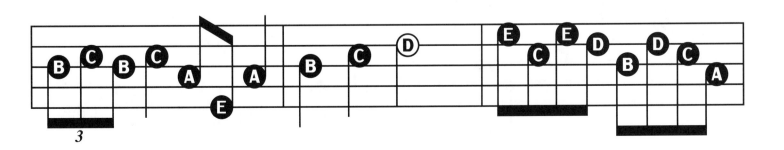

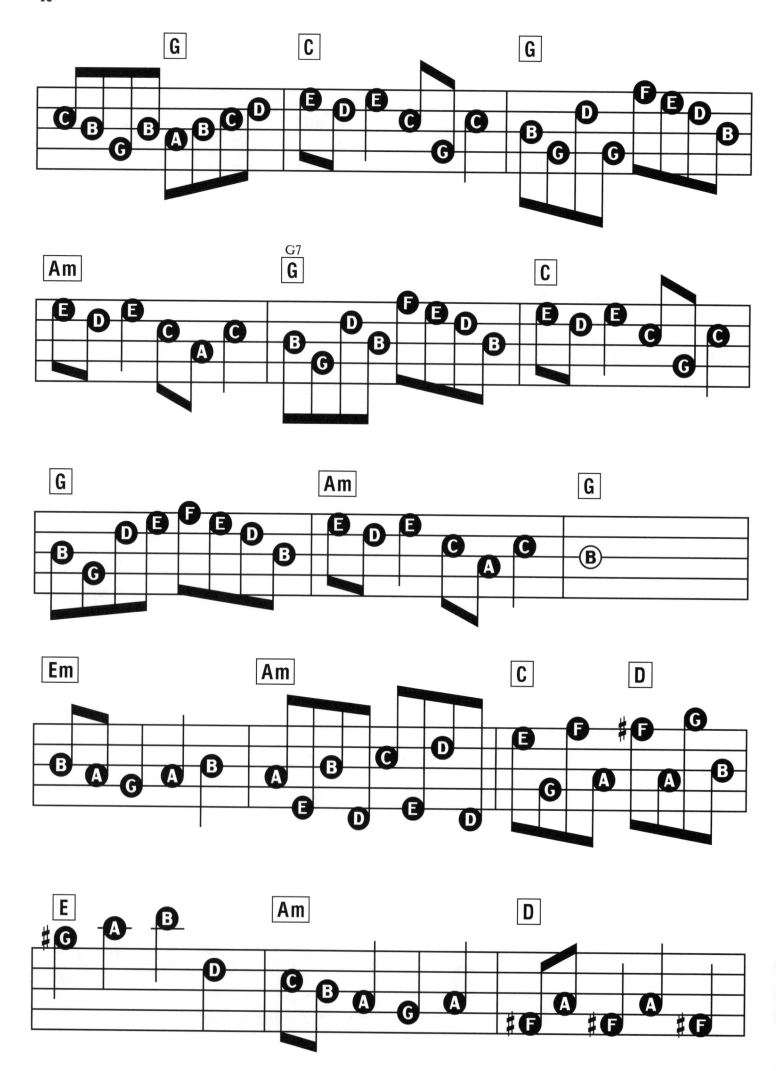

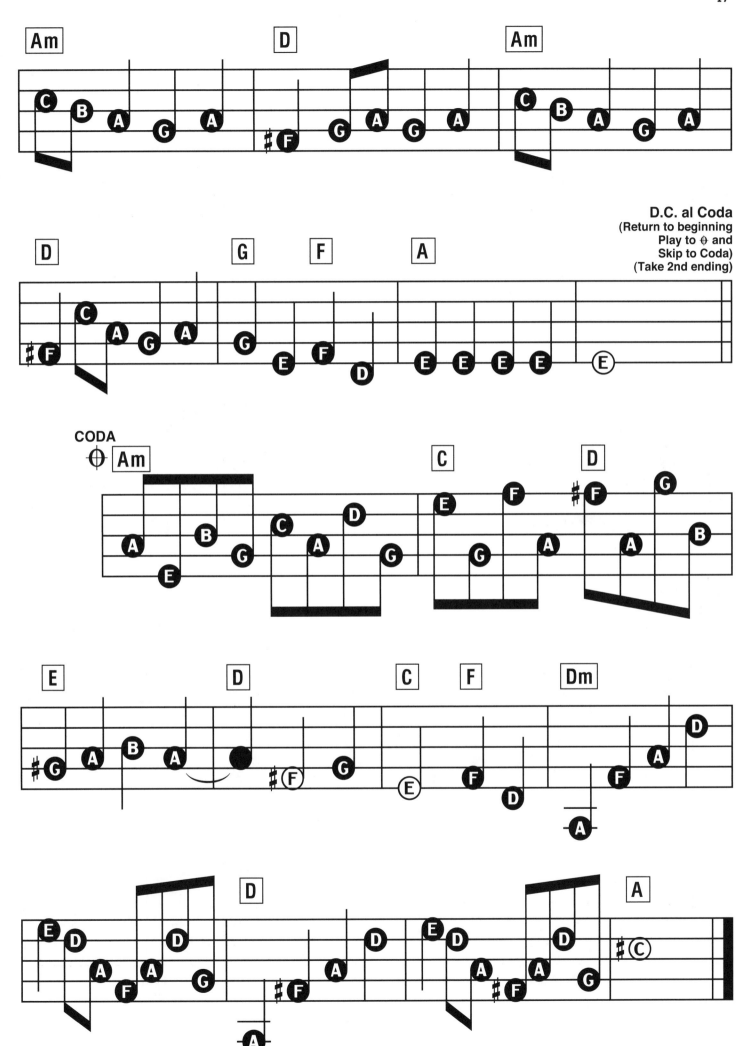

Cissy Strut

Registration 4
Rhythm: Funk or Pop

By Arthur Neville, Leo Nocentelli,
George Porter and Joseph Modeliste, Jr.

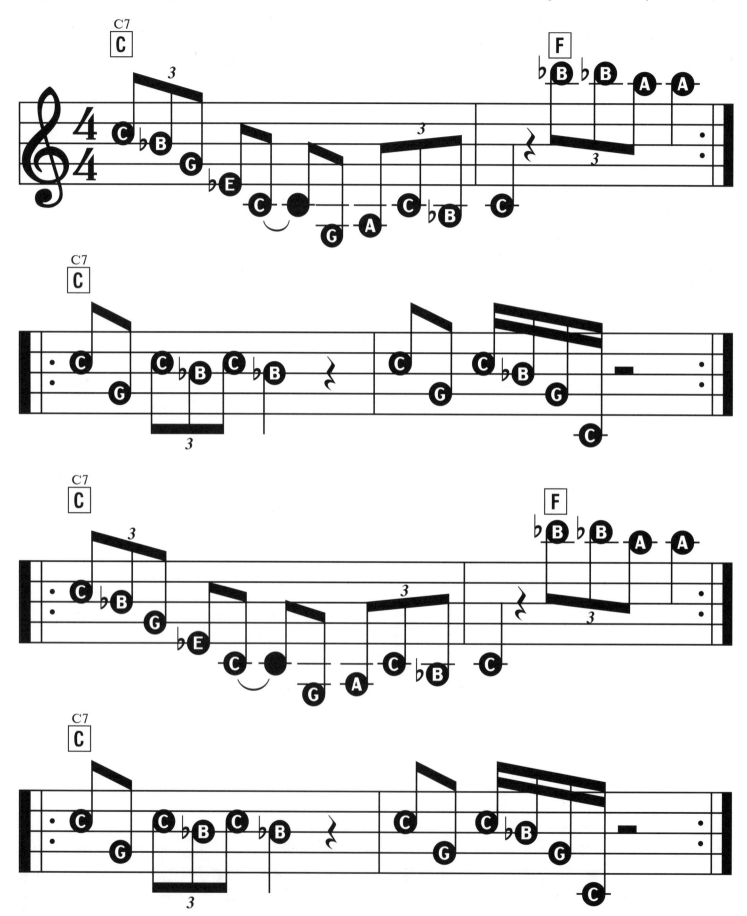

19

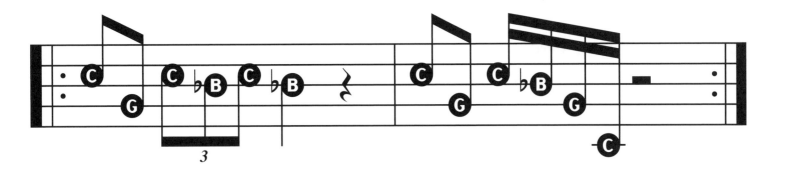

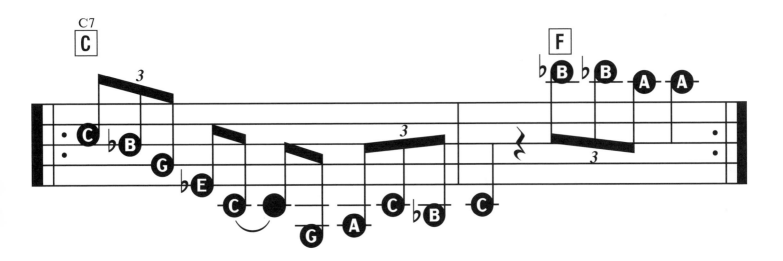

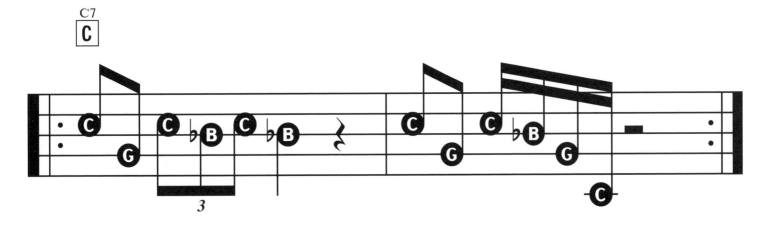

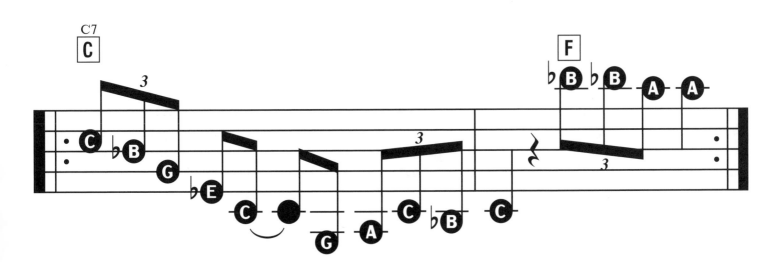

Feels So Good

Registration 2
Rhythm: Latin or Latin Rock

By Chuck Mangione

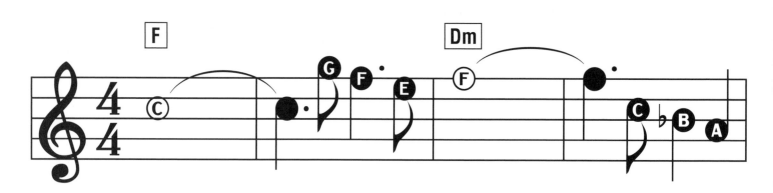

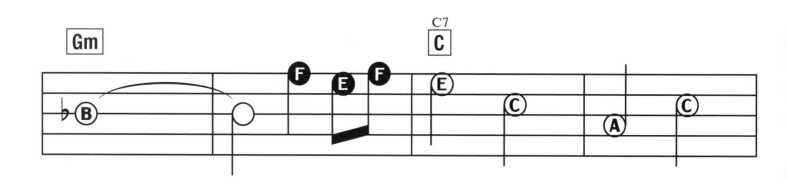

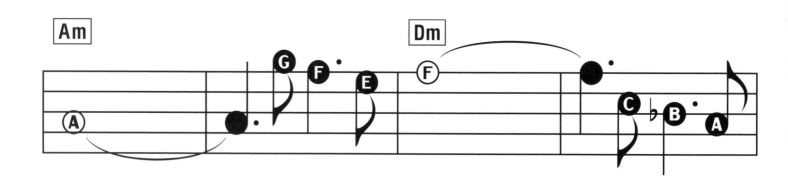

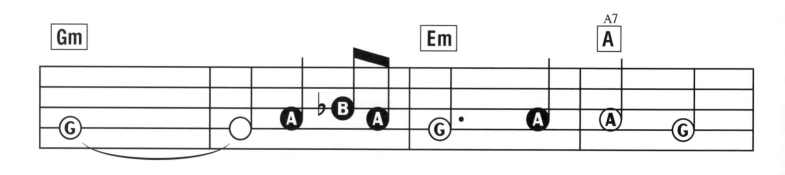

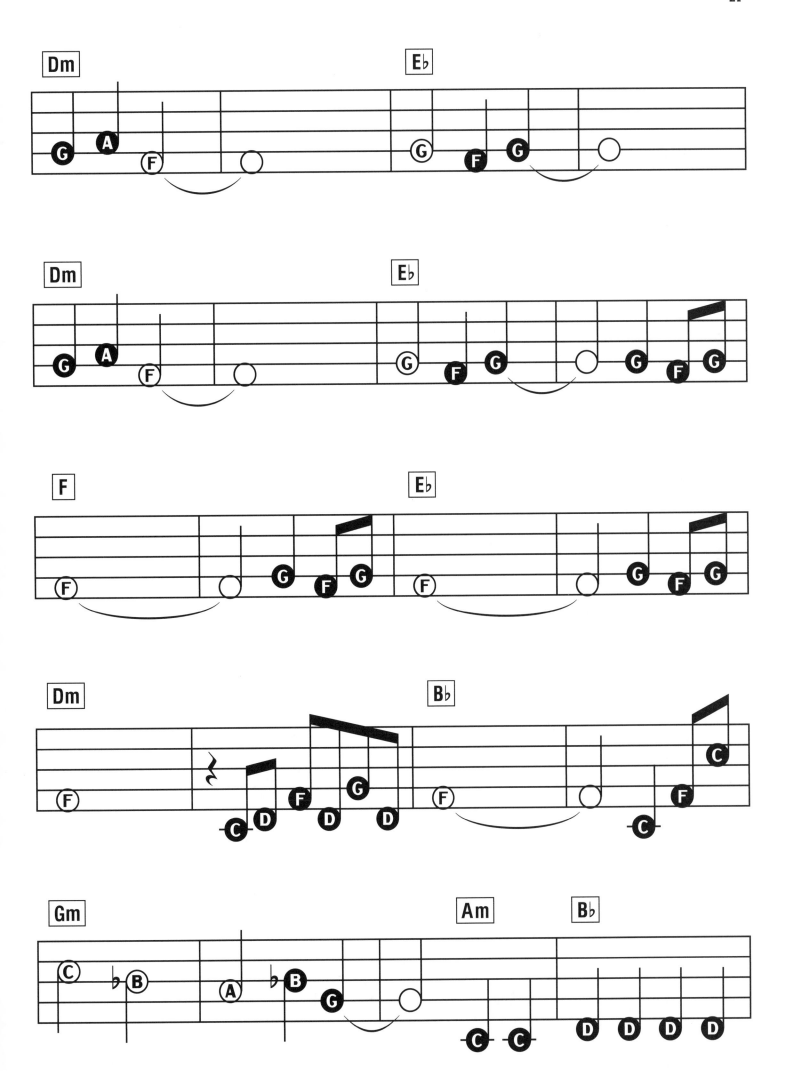

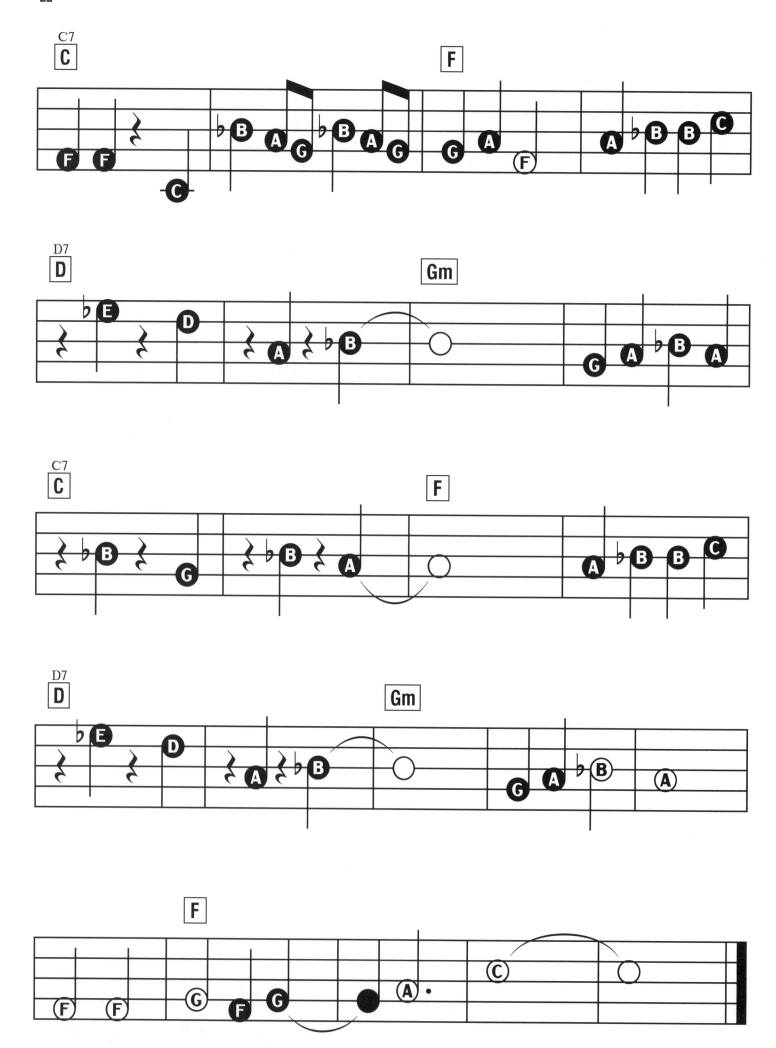

Last Date

Registration 8
Rhythm: Slow Rock or Country Swing

By Floyd Cramer

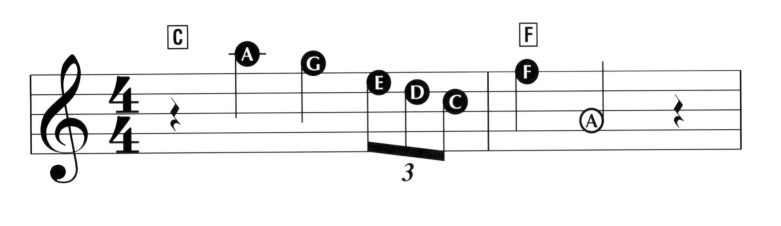

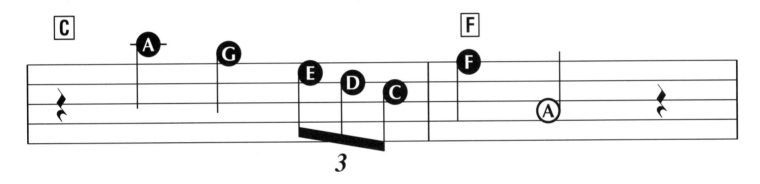

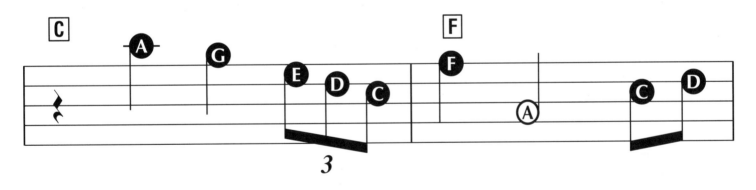

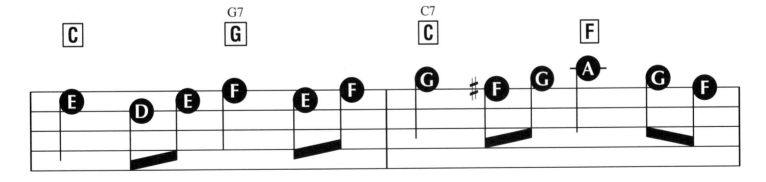

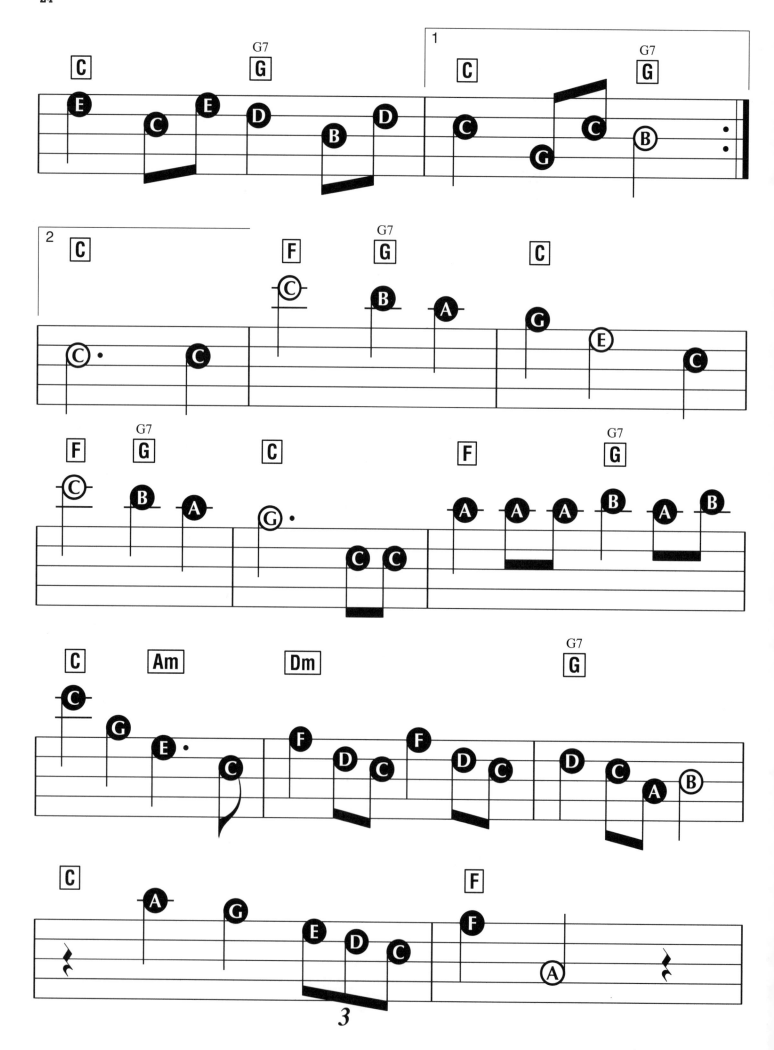

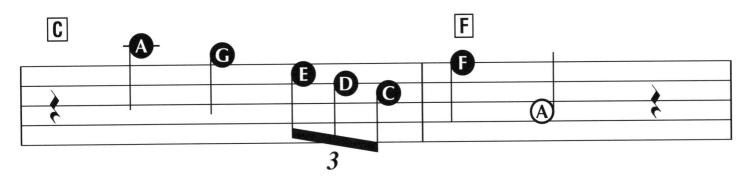

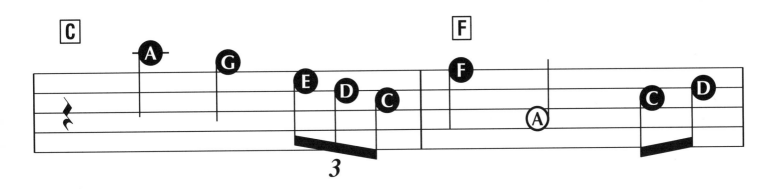

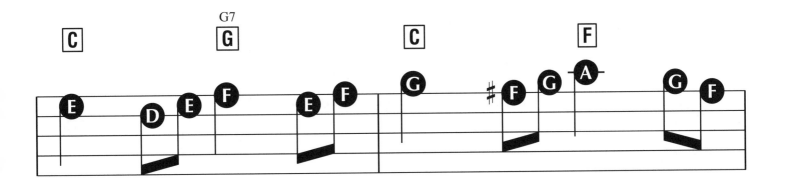

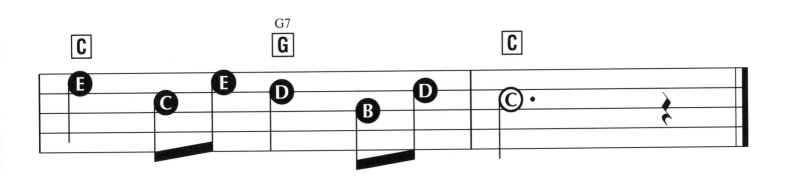

Green Onions

Registration 8
Rhythm: Swing

Written by Al Jackson, Jr.,
Lewis Steinberg, Booker T. Jones
and Steve Cropper

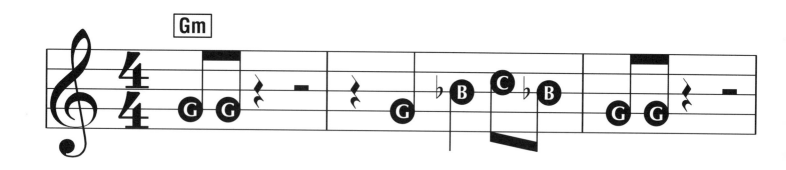

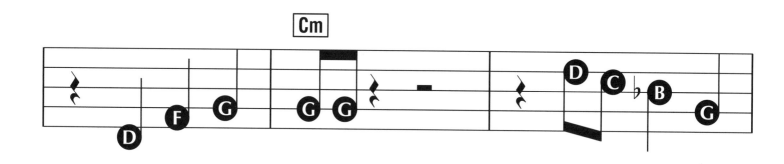

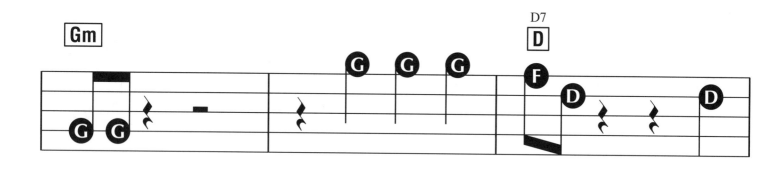

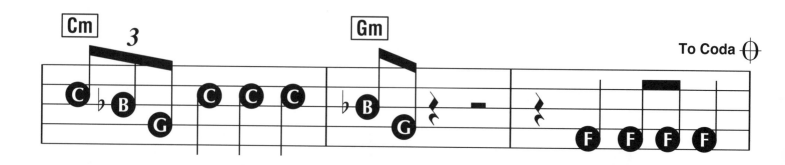

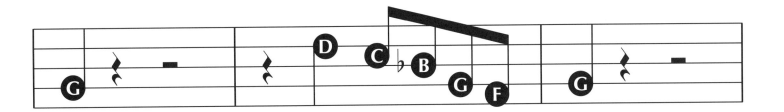

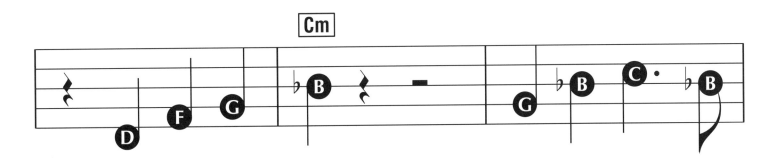

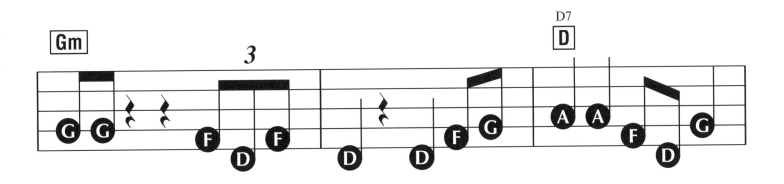

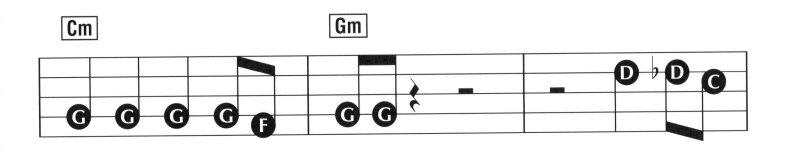

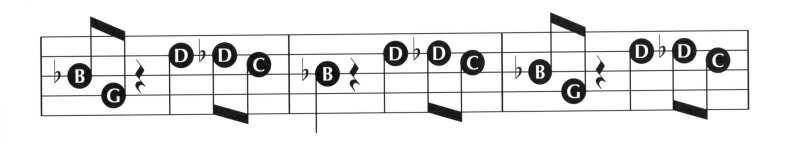

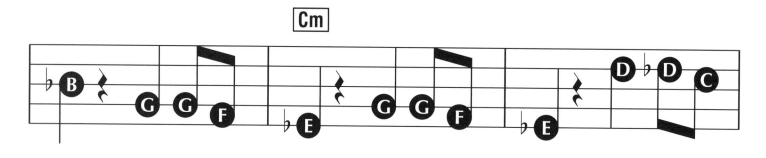

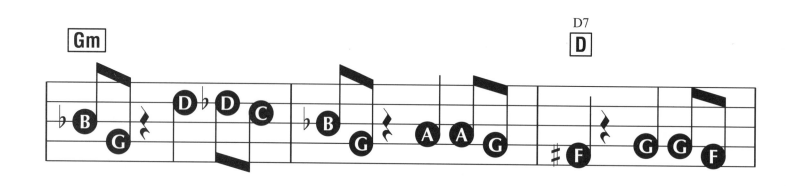

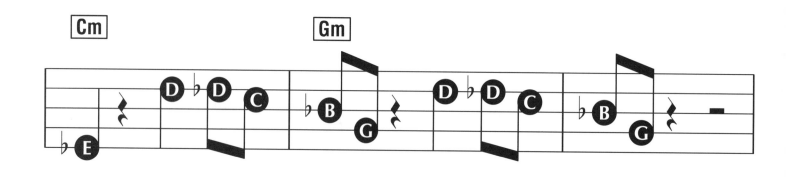

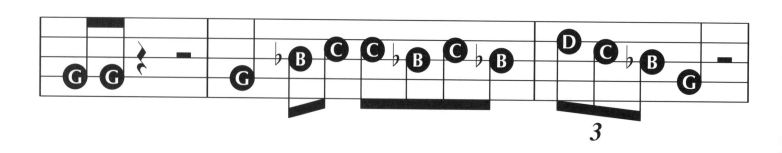

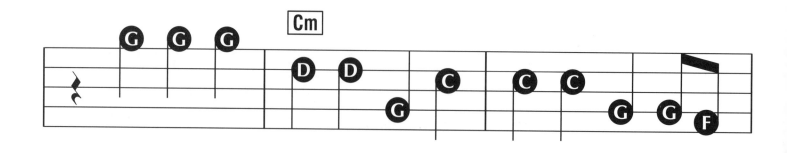

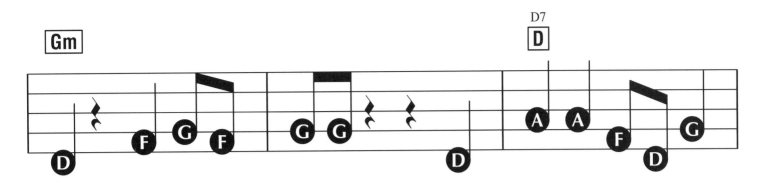

D.C. al Coda
(Return to beginning
Play to ⊕ and
Skip to Coda)

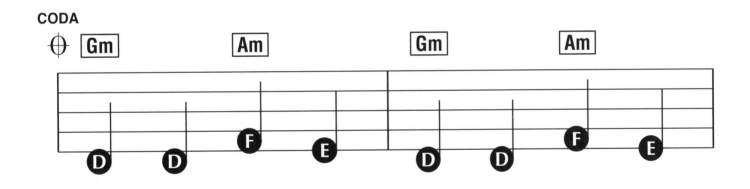

CODA

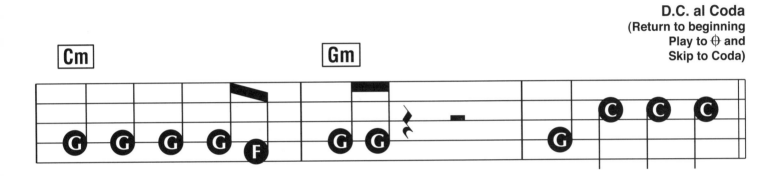

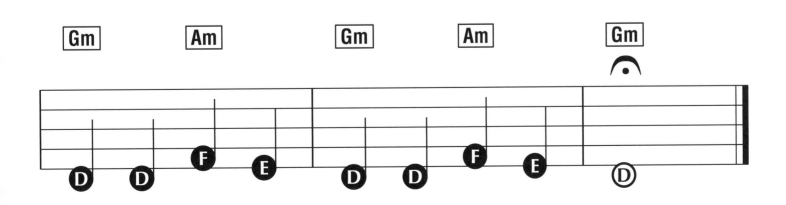

The Happy Organ

Registration 2
Rhythm: Rock 'n' Roll or Swing

By Ken Wood, David Clowney
and James Kriegsmann

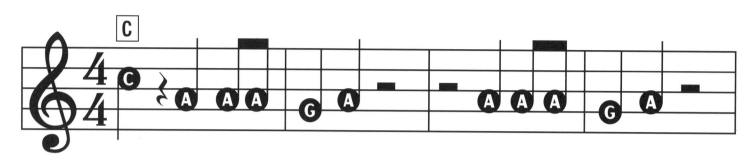

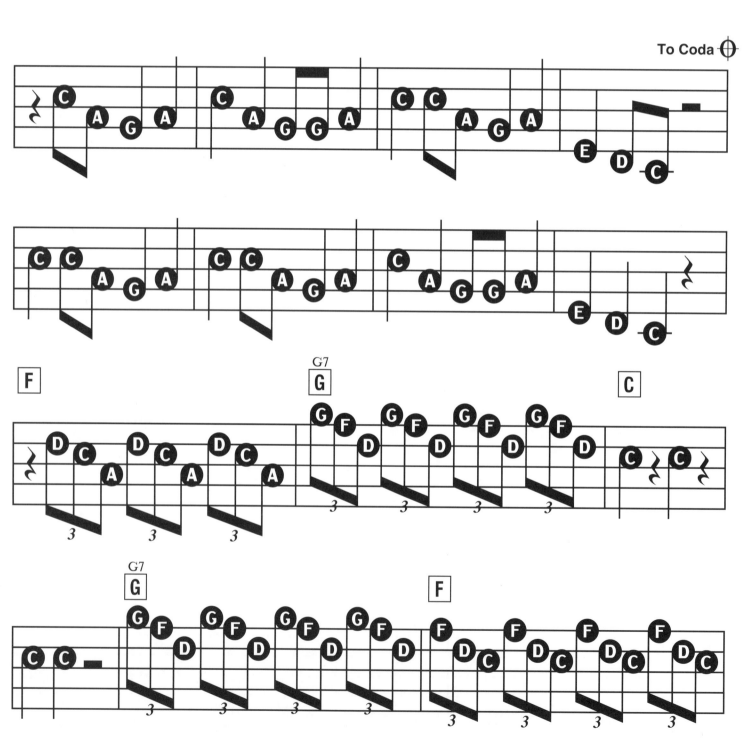

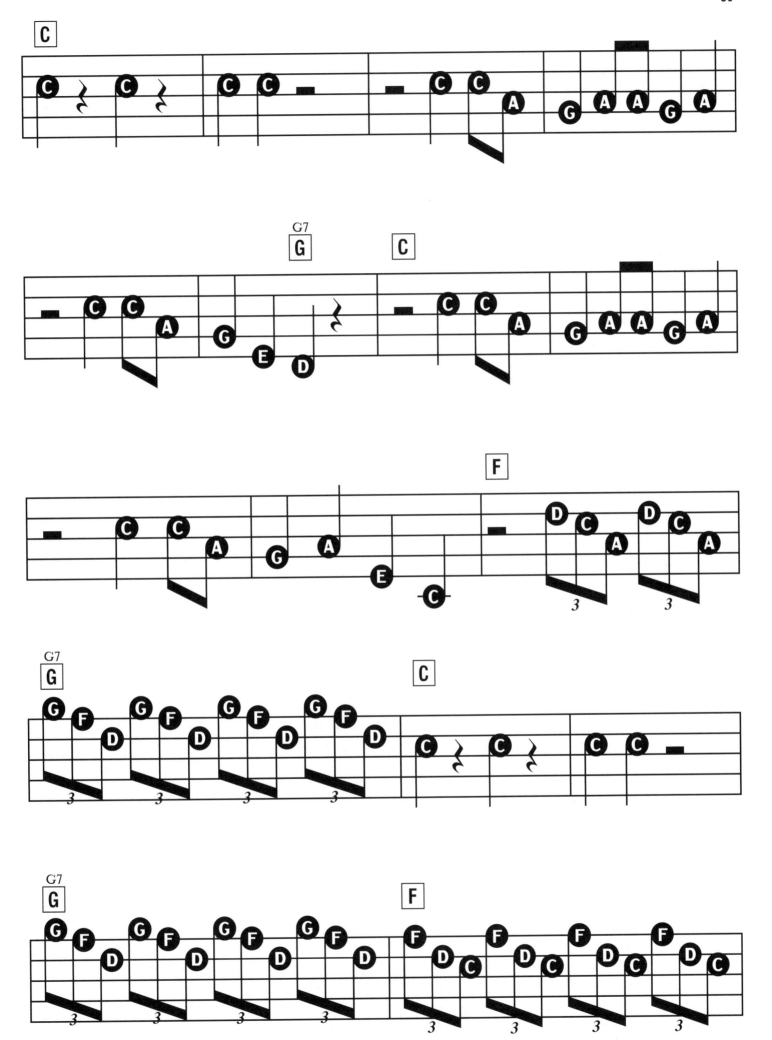

32

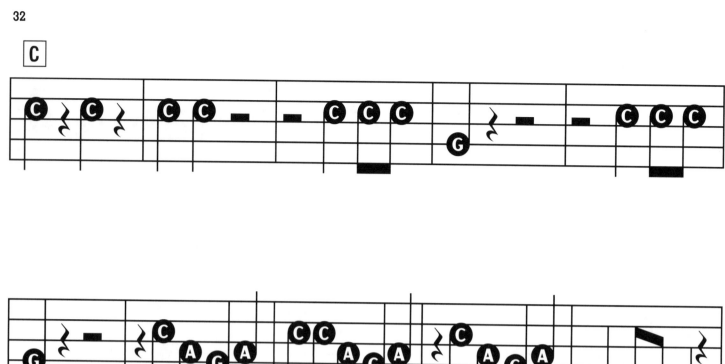

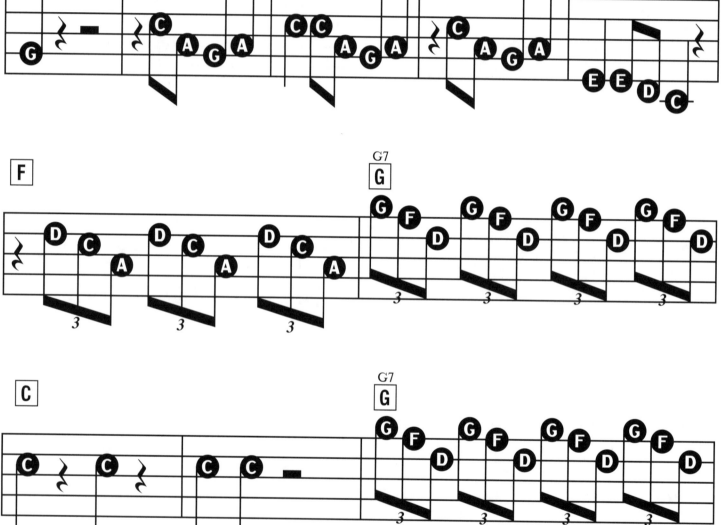

D.C. al Coda
(Return to beginning
Play to ⊕ and
Skip to Coda)

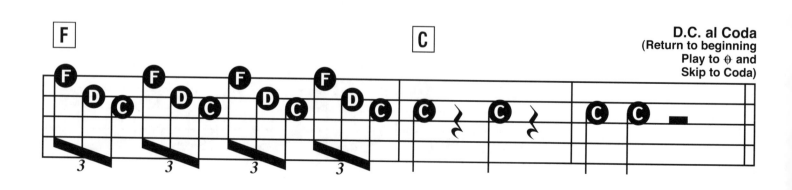

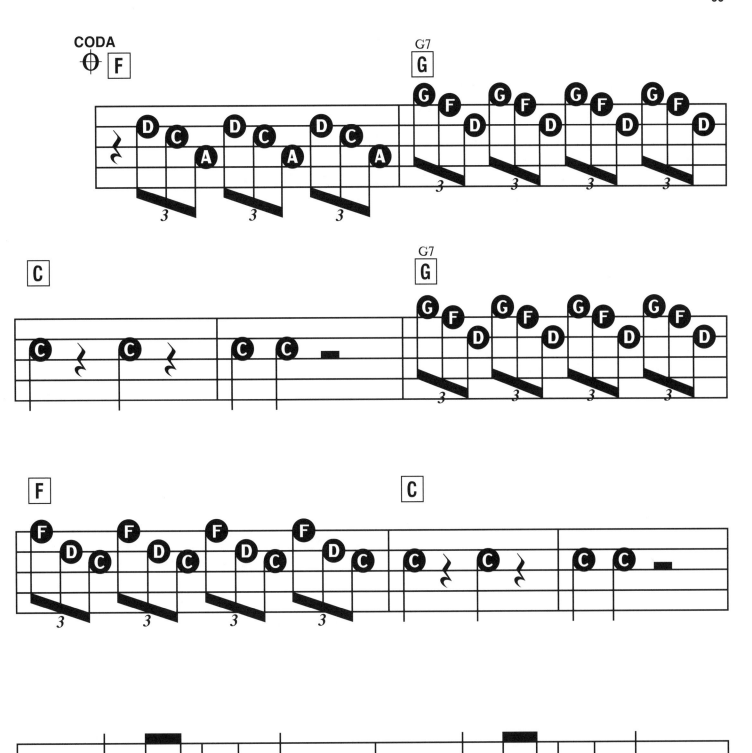

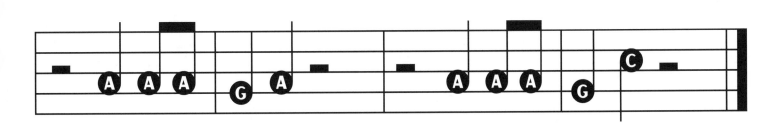

Hawaii Five-O
from the Television Series

Registration 2
Rhythm: Jazz Rock

By Mort Stevens

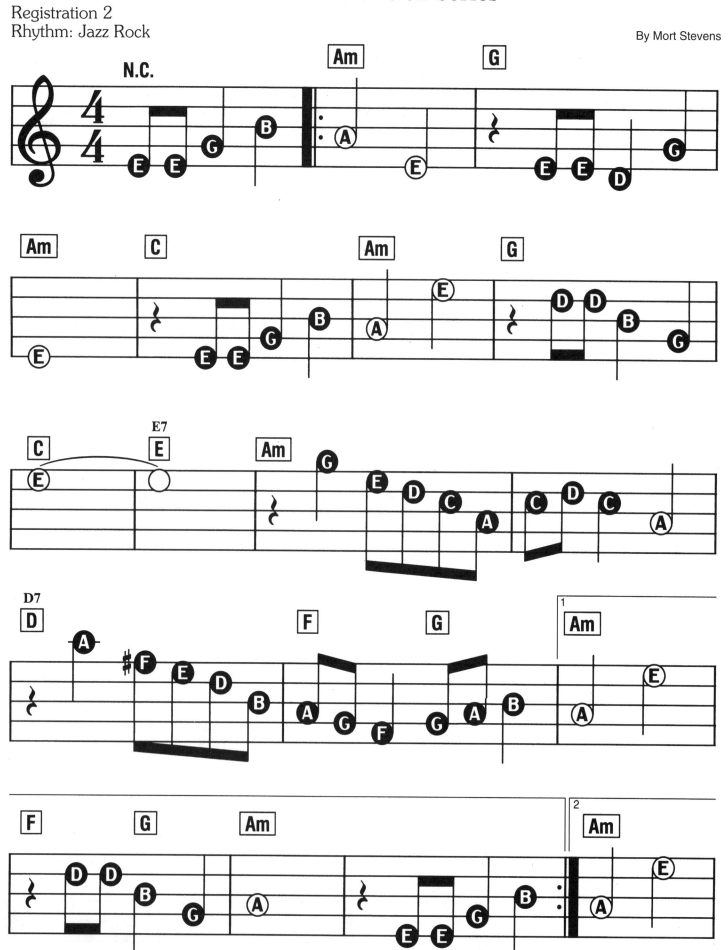

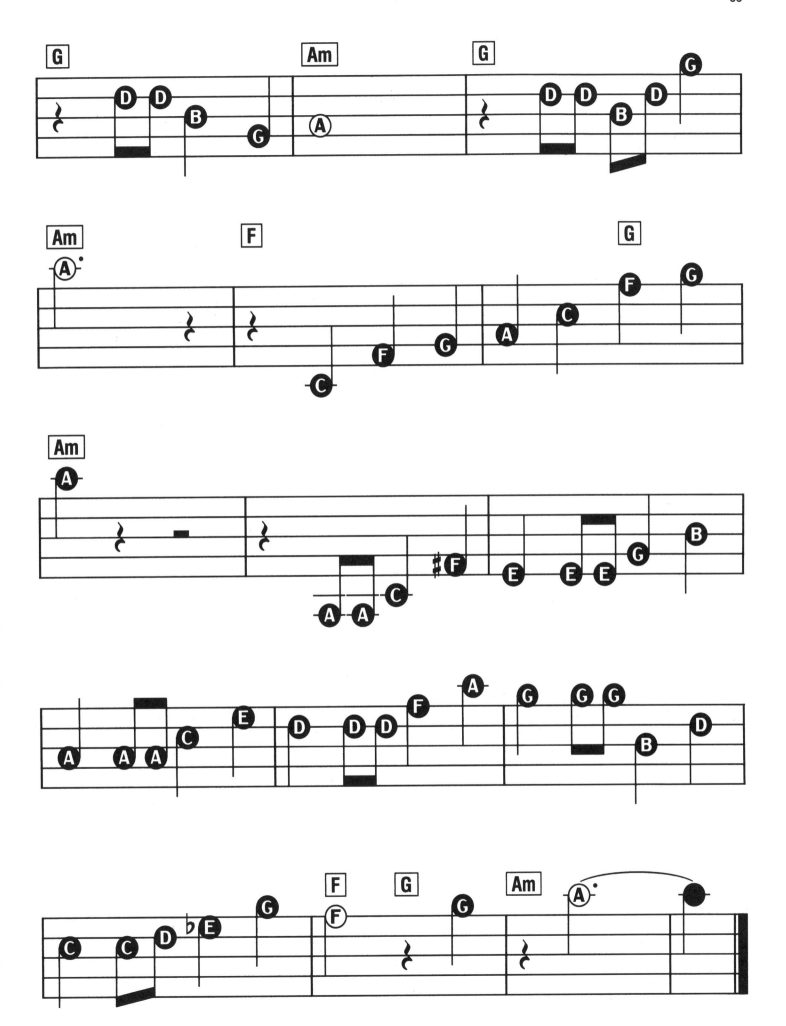

Honky Tonk
(Parts 1 & 2)

Registration 4
Rhythm: Blues or Shuffle

Words and Music by Berisford "Shep" Shepherd,
Clifford Scott, Bill Doggett and Billy Butler

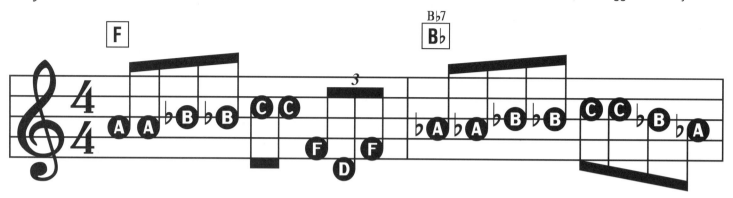

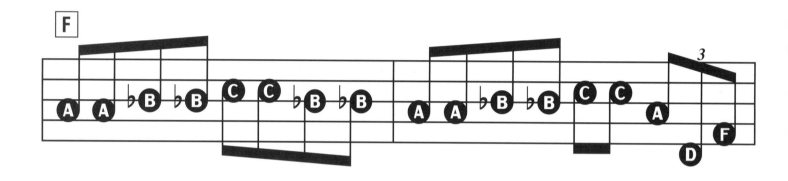

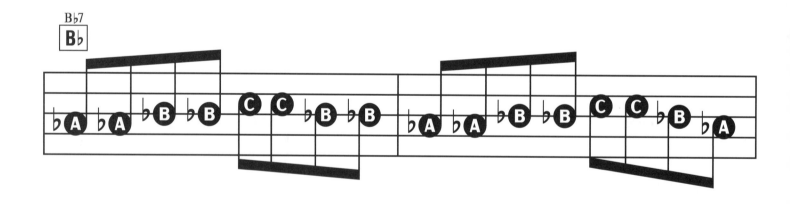

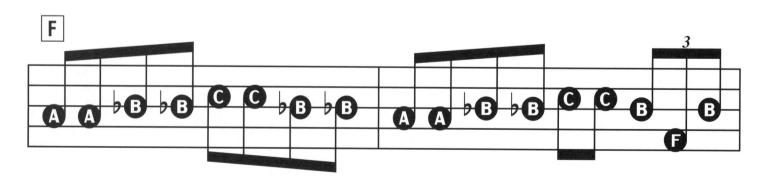

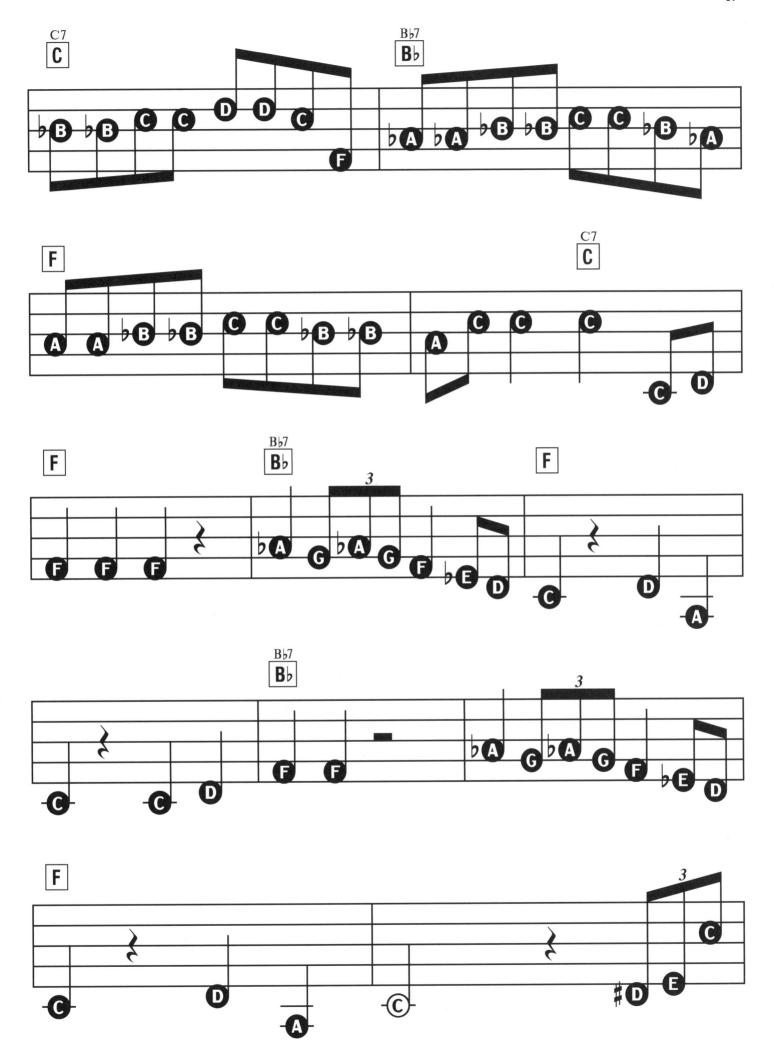

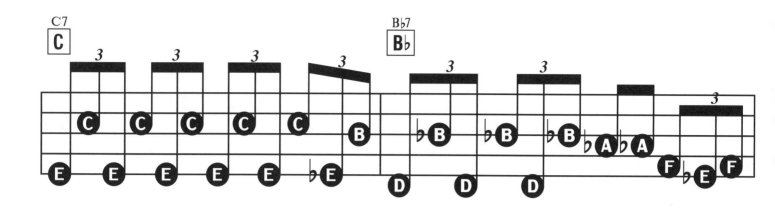

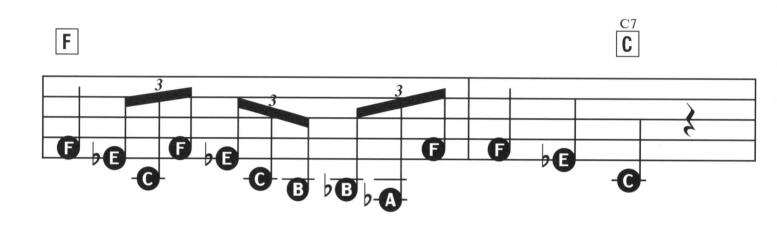

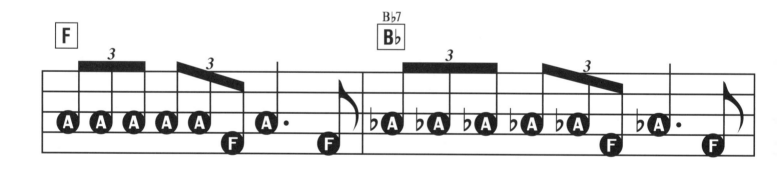

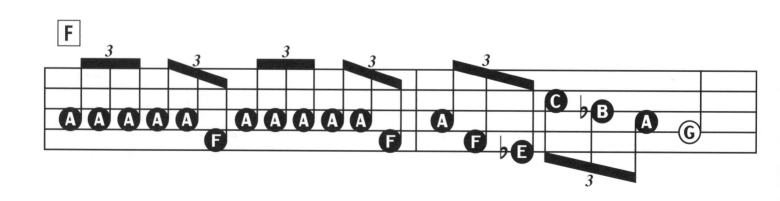

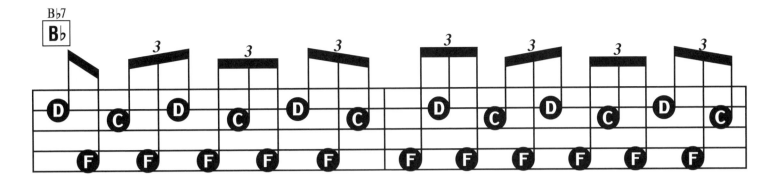

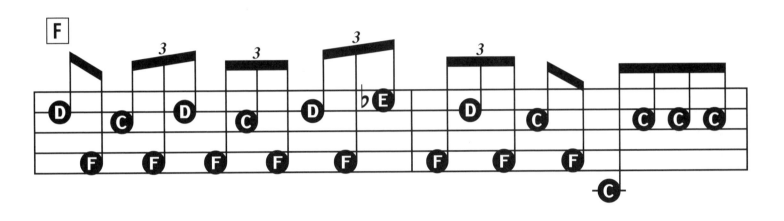

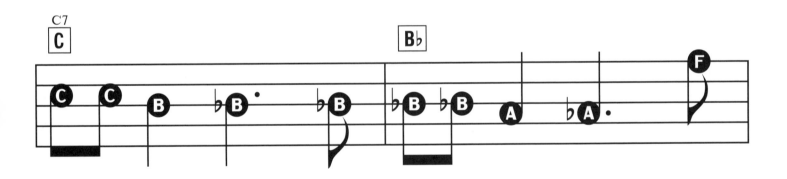

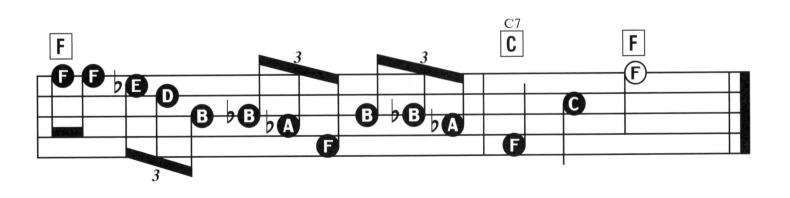

Love Is Blue
(L'amour est bleu)

English Lyric by Bryan Blackburn
Original French Lyric by Pierre Cour
Music by Andre Popp

Registration 1
Rhythm: Ballad

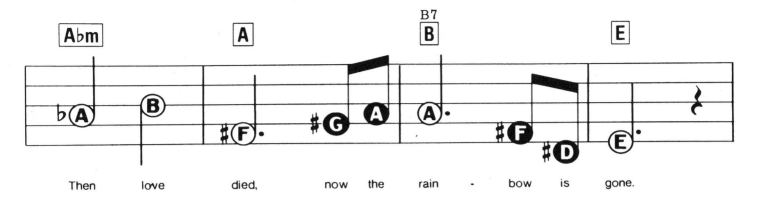

Then   love   died,   now the   rain - bow is   gone.

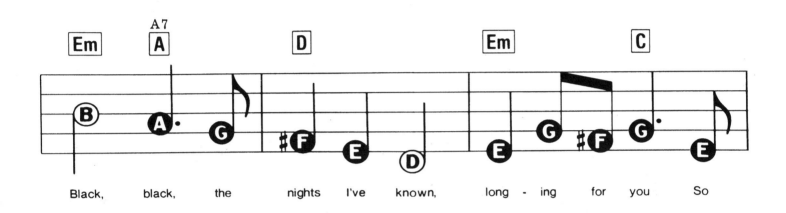

Black,   black,   the   nights I've   known,   long - ing for you So

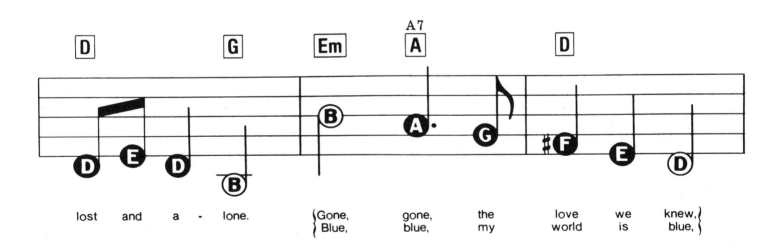

lost and a - lone.   {Gone,   gone,   the   love   we   knew,}
{Blue,   blue,   my   world   is   blue,}

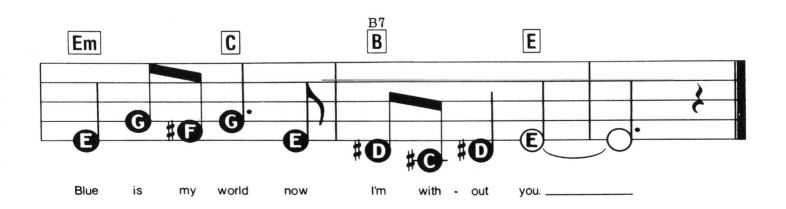

Blue is my world now   I'm with - out you. _____

Midnight in Moscow

Registration 2
Rhythm: Dixieland or Swing

Based on a song by Vassili Soloviev-Sedoy and M. Matusovsky
New Music by Kenny Ball

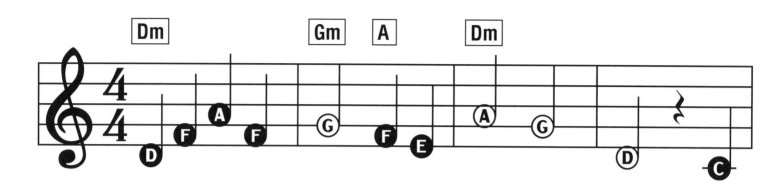

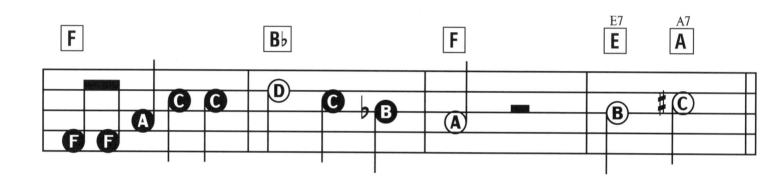

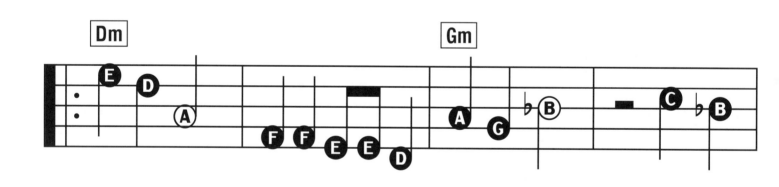

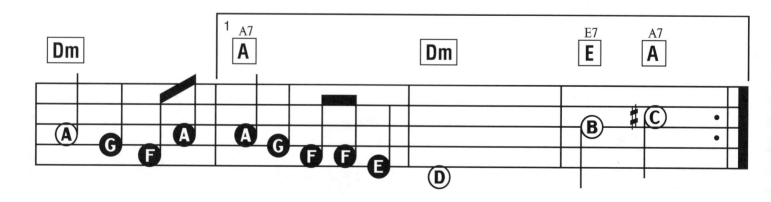

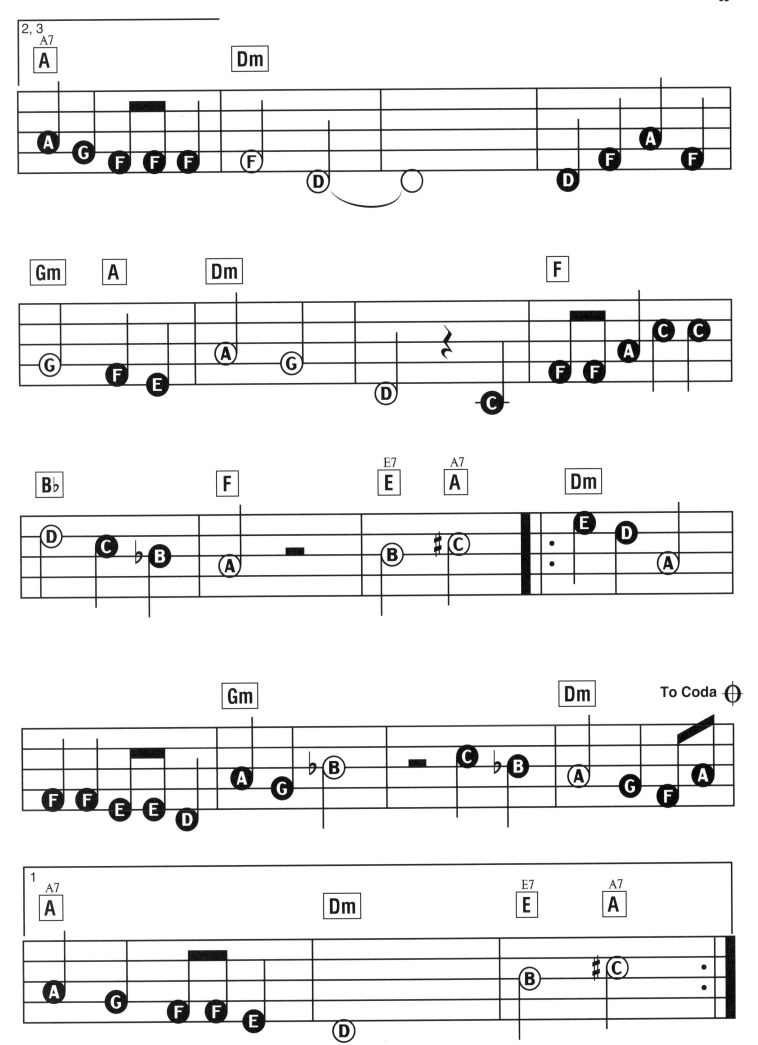

44

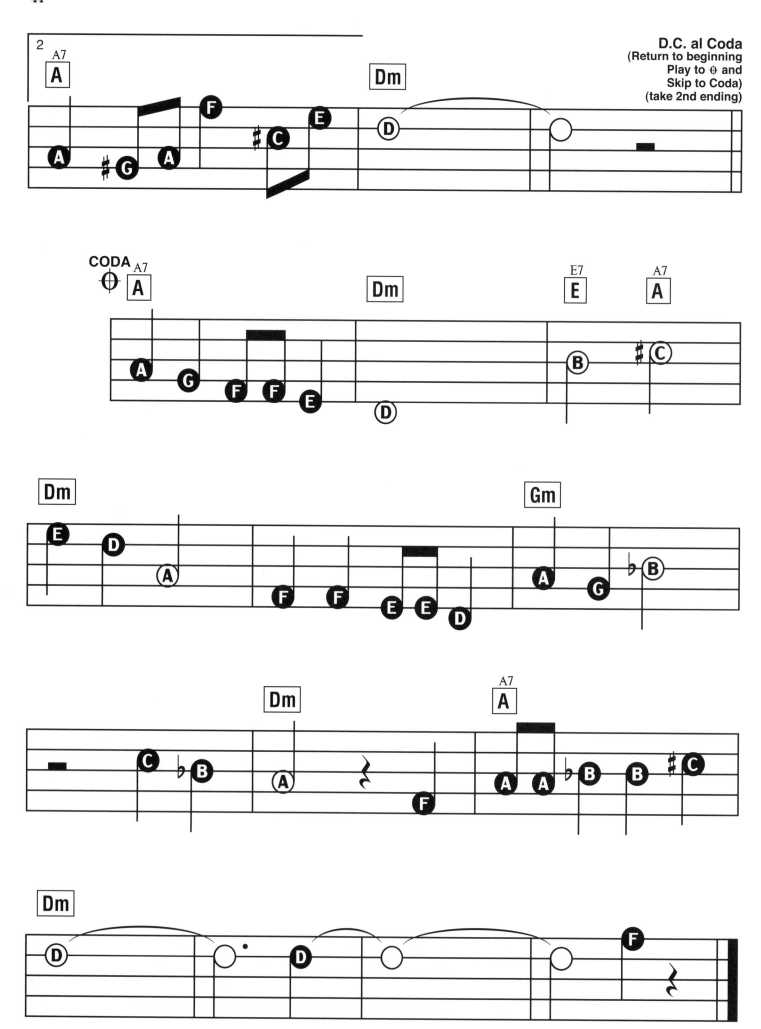

Misirlou

Registration 4
Rhythm: Latin or Rhumba

Words by Fred Wise, Milton Leeds,
Jose Pina and Sidney Russell
Music by Nicolas Roubanis

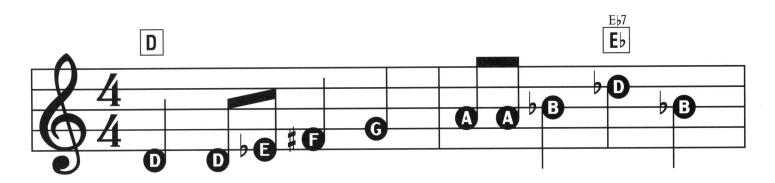

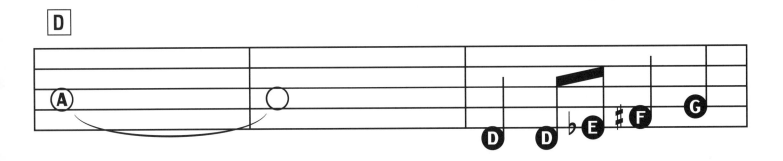

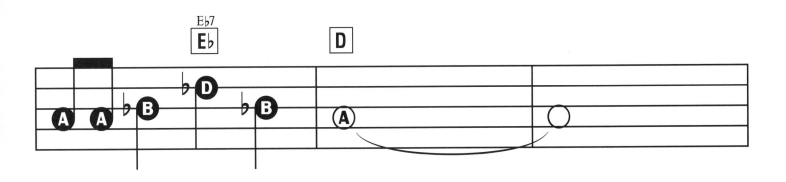

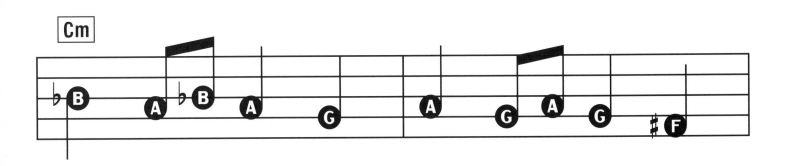

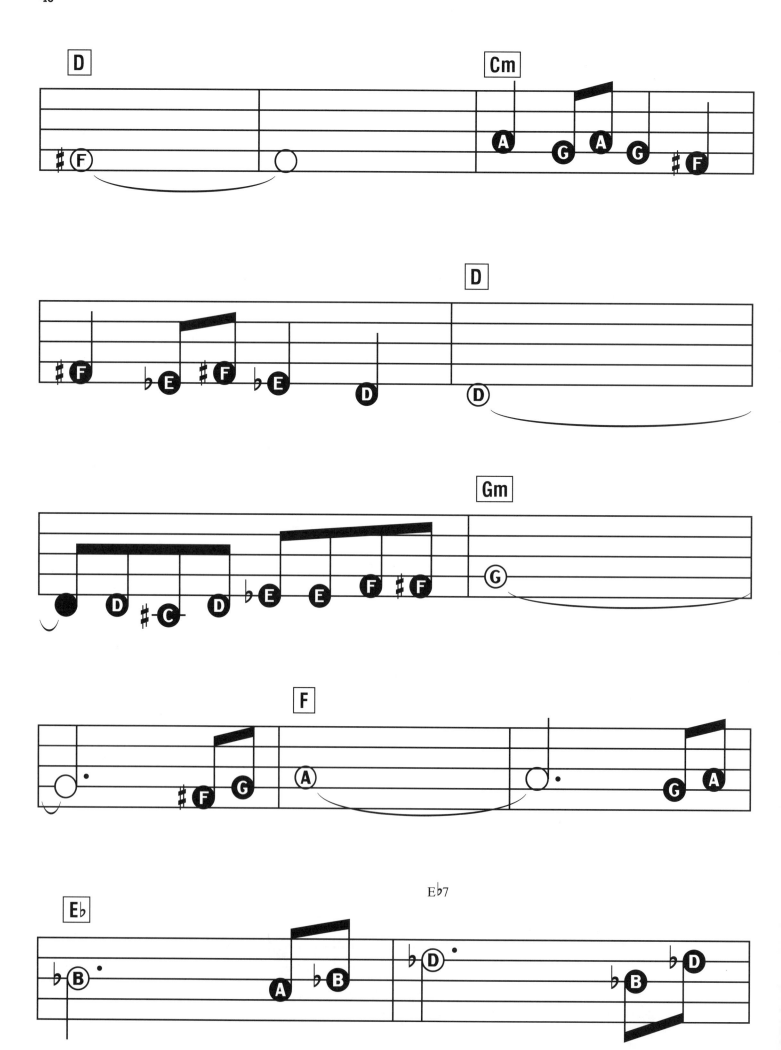

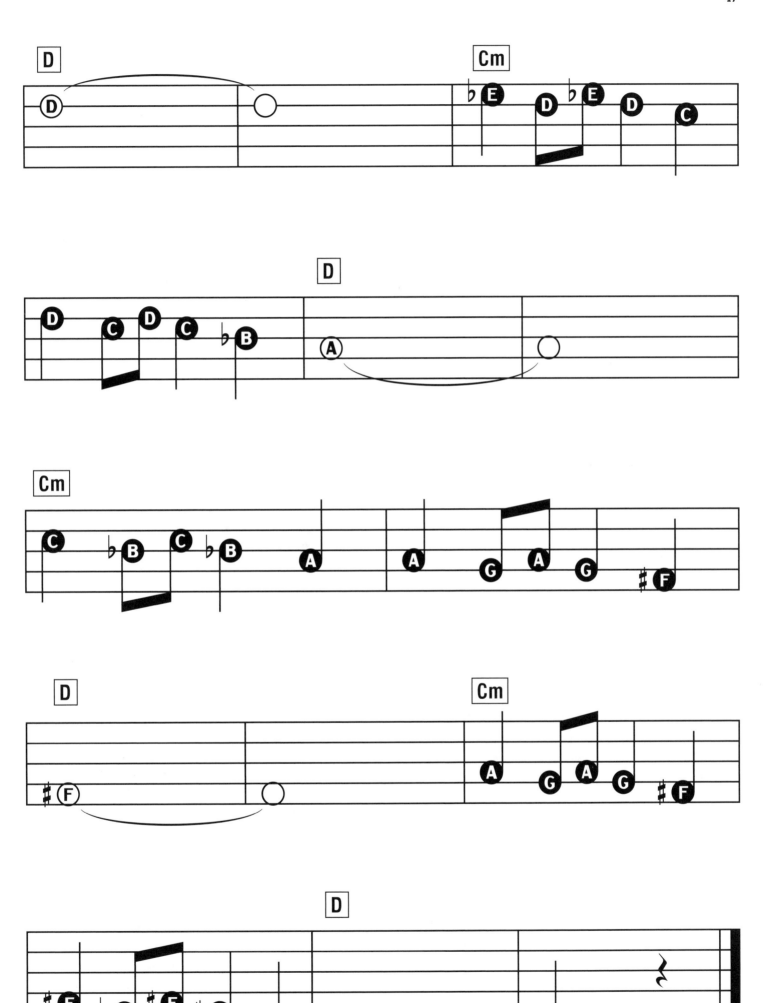

Mission: Impossible Theme
from the Paramount Television Series MISSION: IMPOSSIBLE

Registration 2
Rhythm: Jazz Waltz or Waltz

By Lalo Schifrin

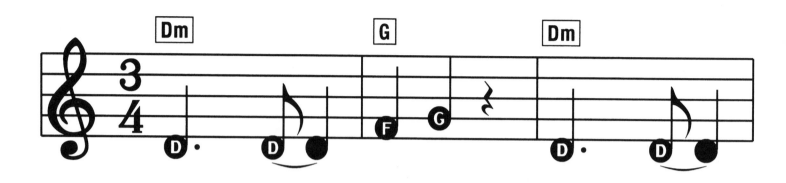

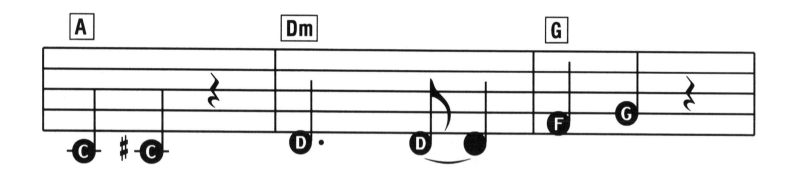

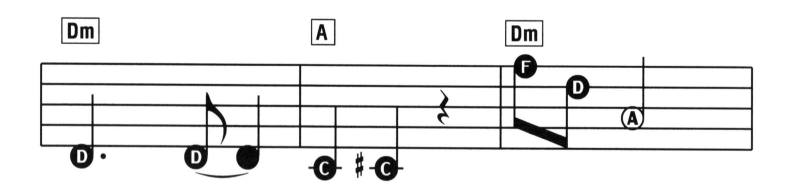

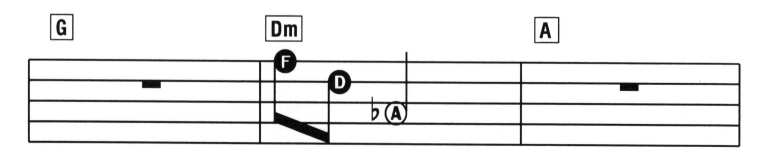

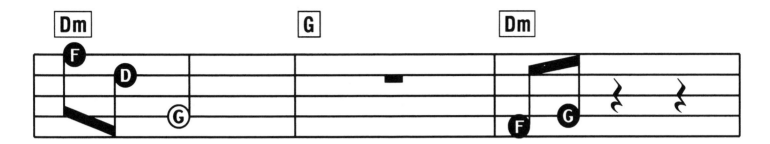
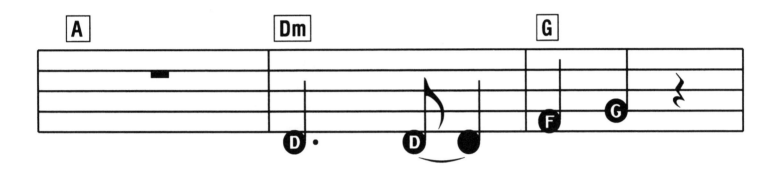
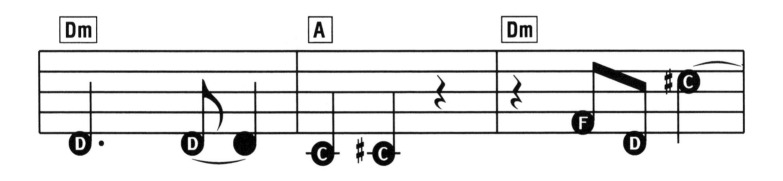
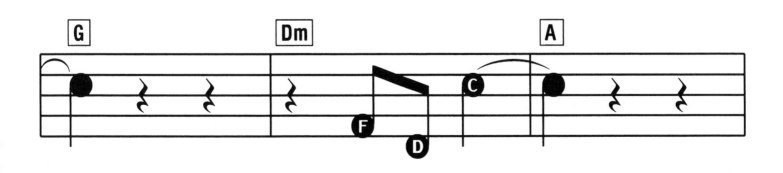

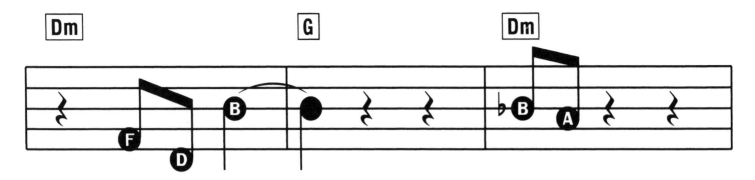

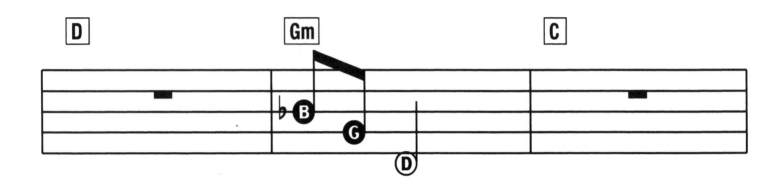

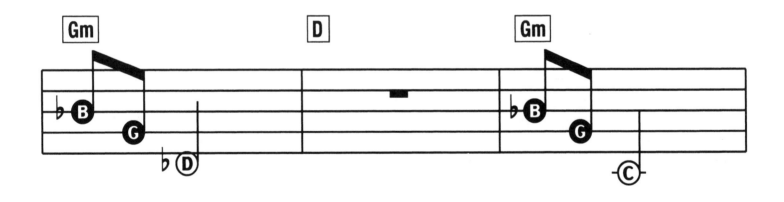

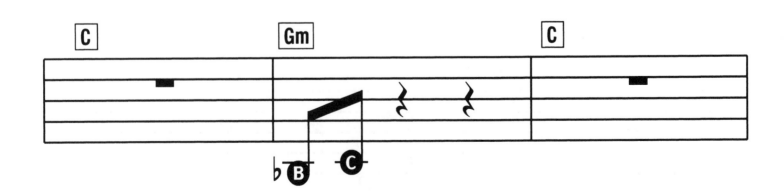

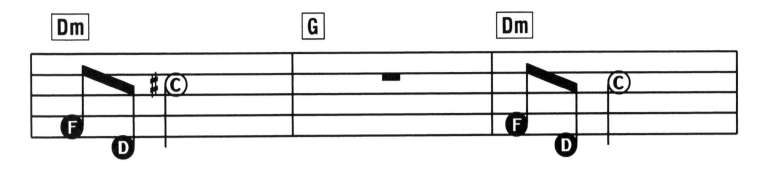

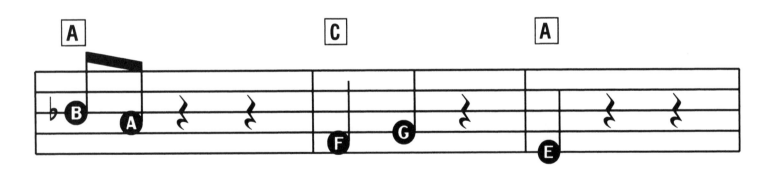

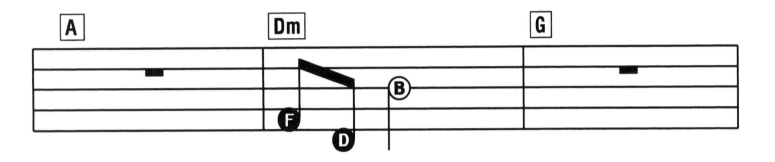

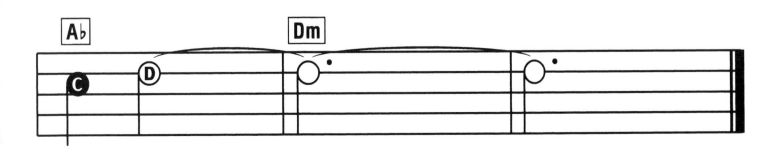

Peter Gunn
Theme Song from the Television Series

Registration 3
Rhythm: Rock

By Henry Mancini

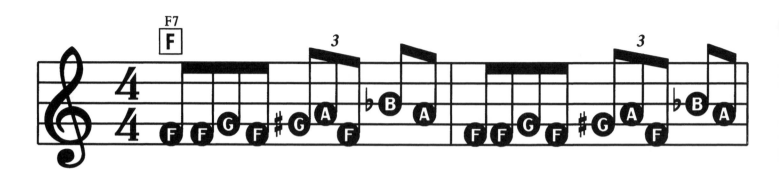

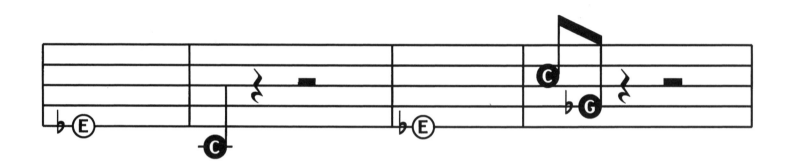

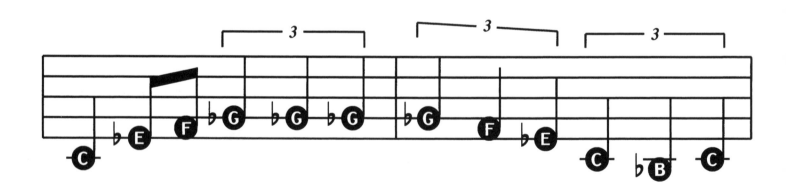

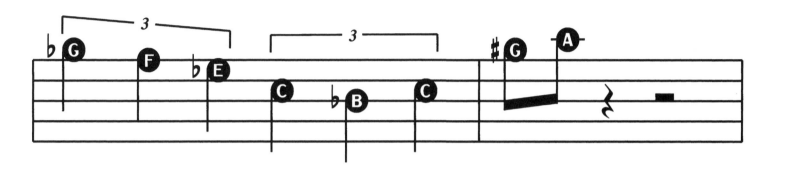

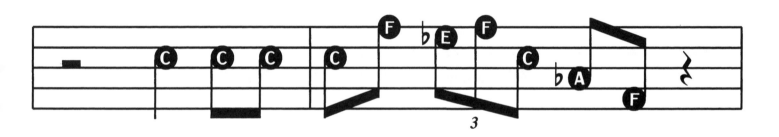

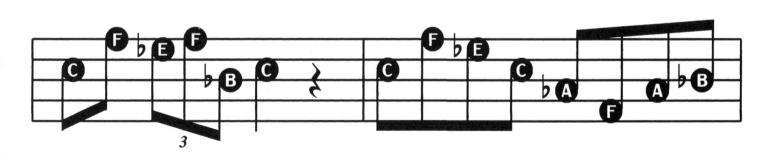

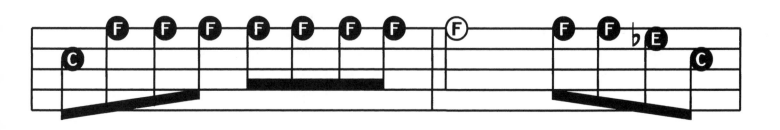

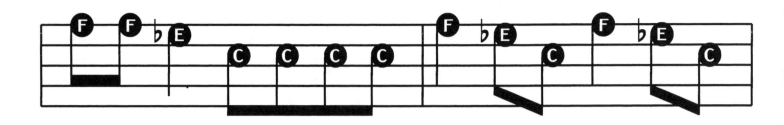

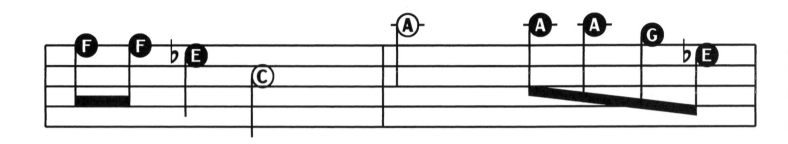

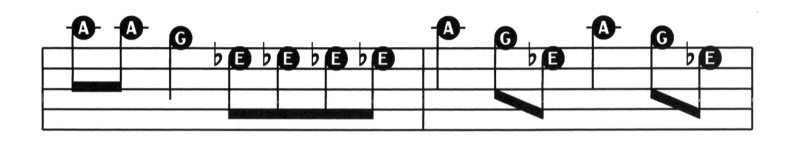

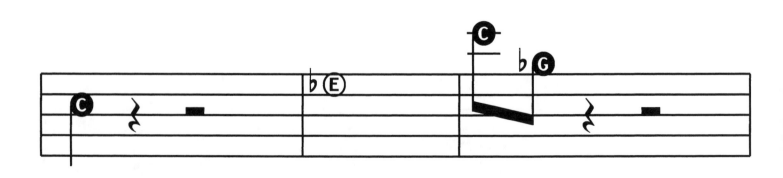

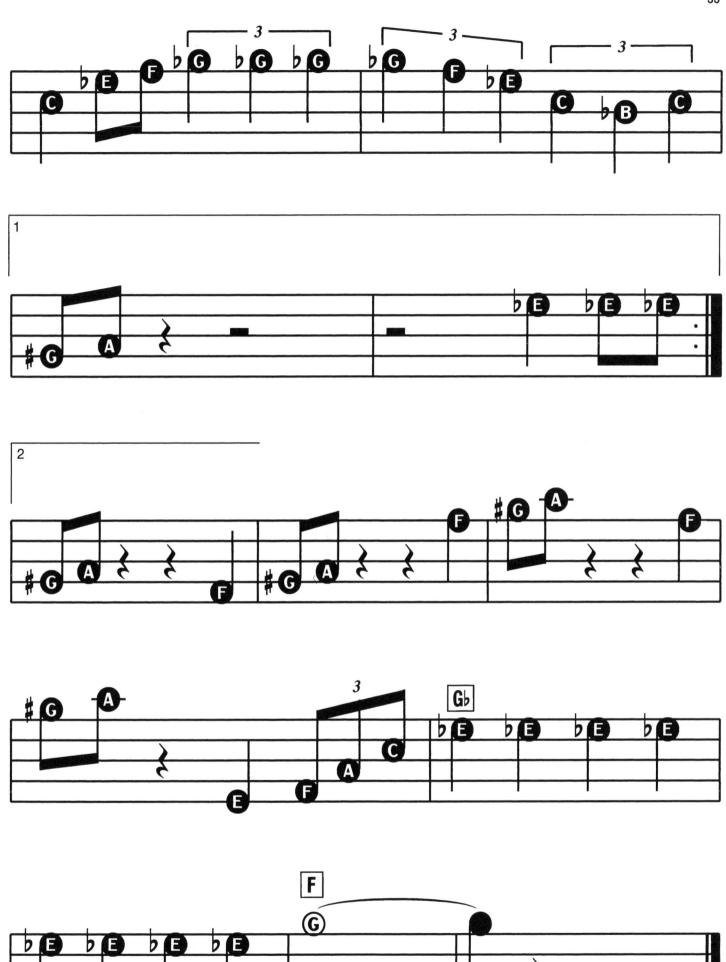

The Pink Panther
from THE PINK PANTHER

Registration 1
Rhythm: Swing

By Henry Mancini

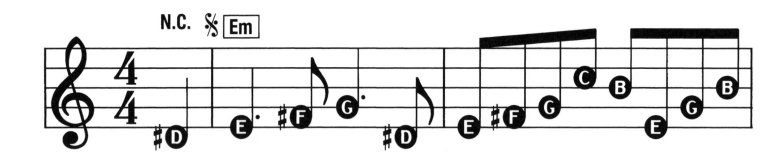

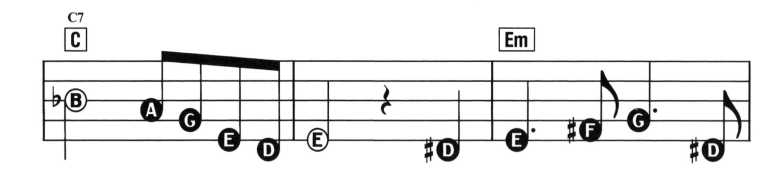

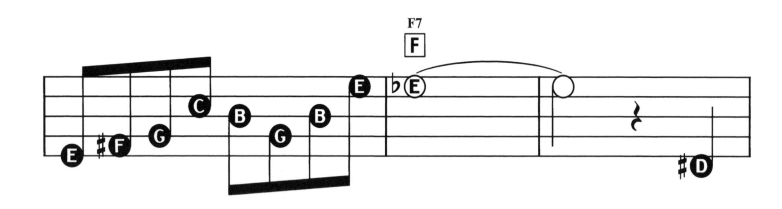

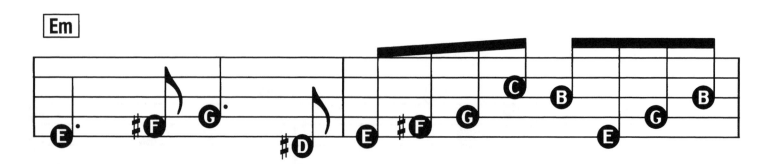

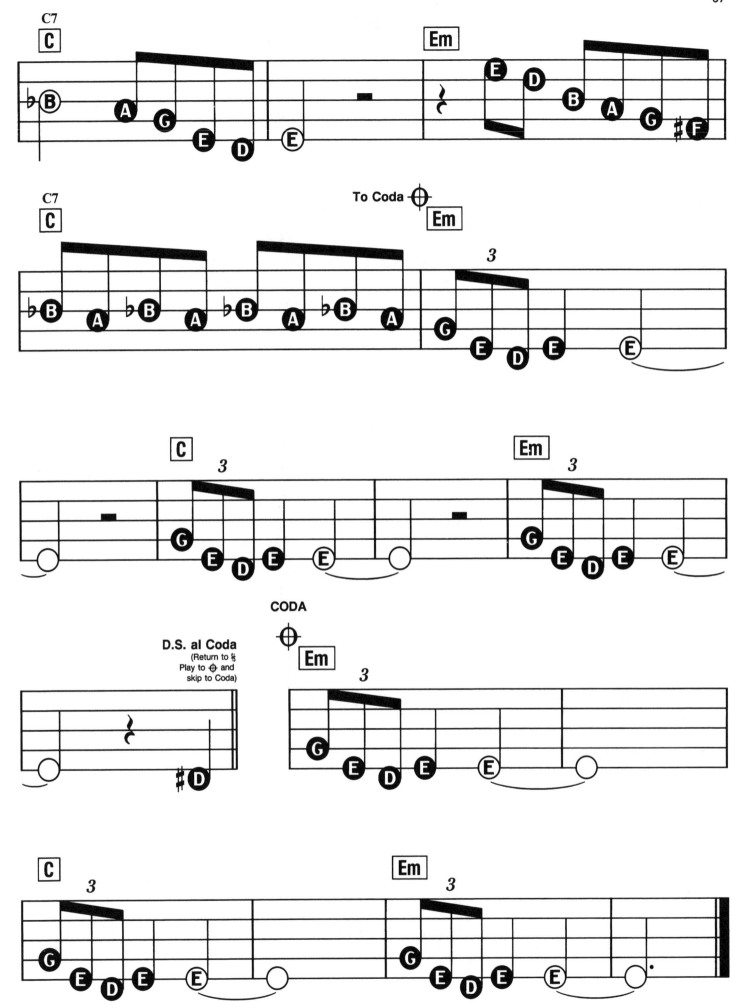

Pipeline

Registration 4
Rhythm: Rock

By Bob Spickard
and Brian Carman

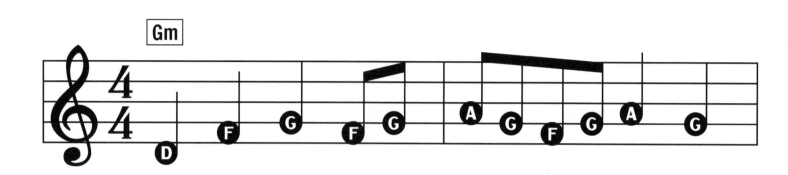

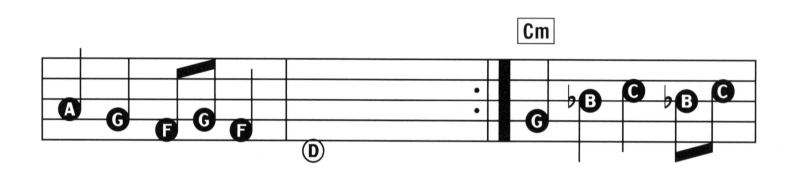

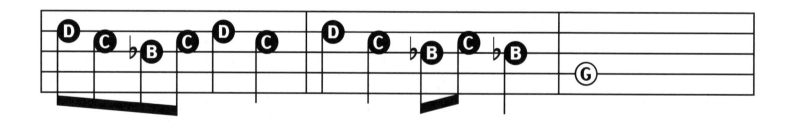

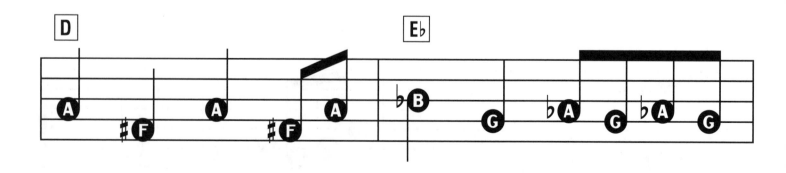

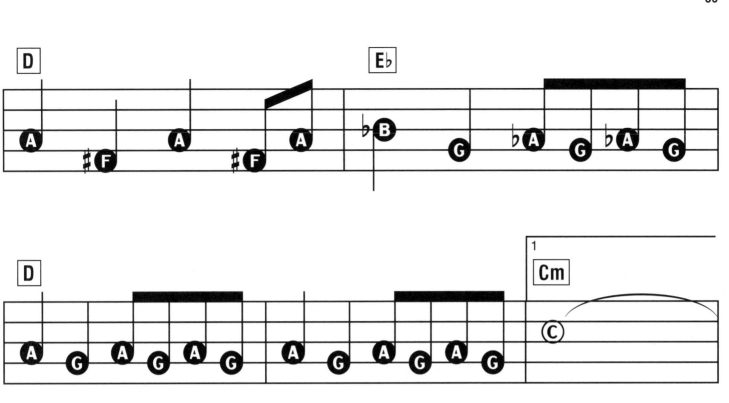

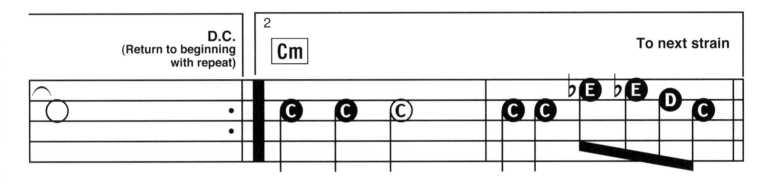

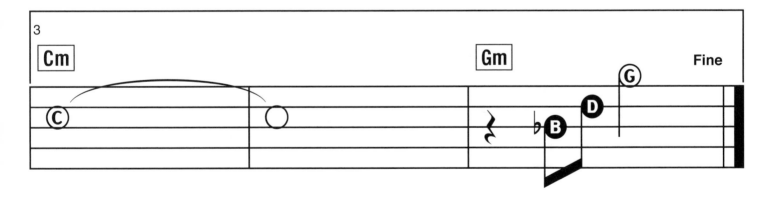

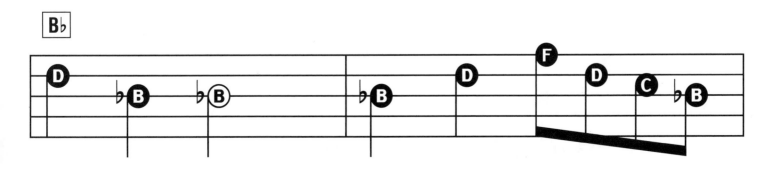

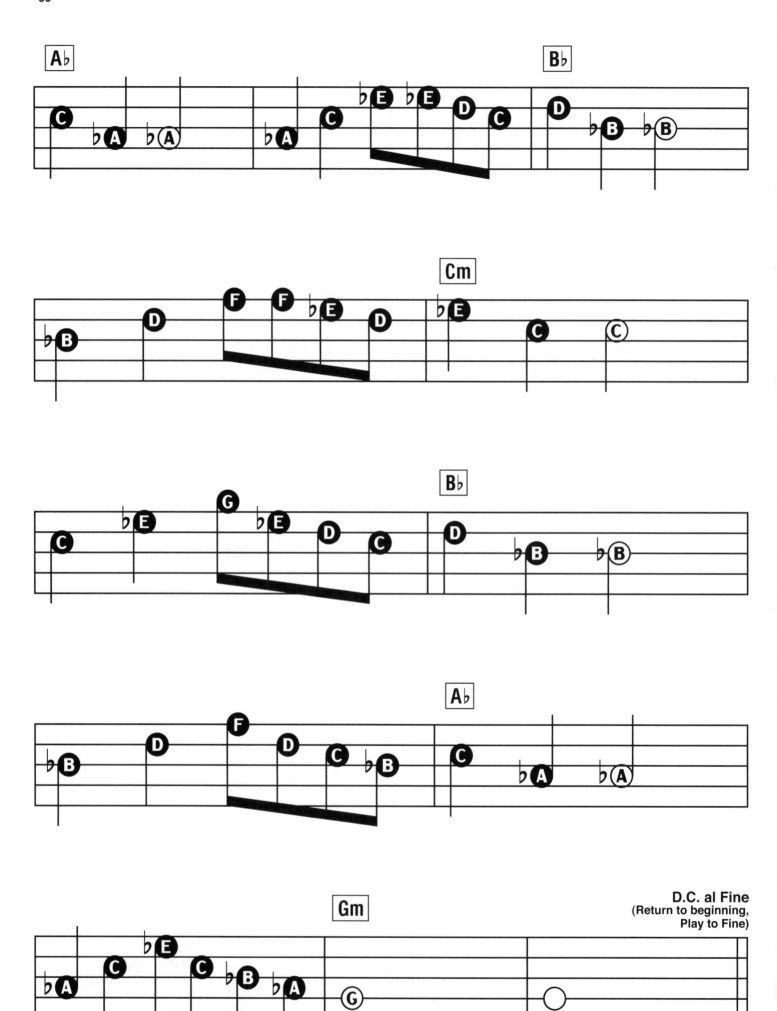

D.C. al Fine
(Return to beginning,
Play to Fine)

Tequila

Registration 10
Rhythm: Latin Rock or Fox Trot

By Chuck Rio

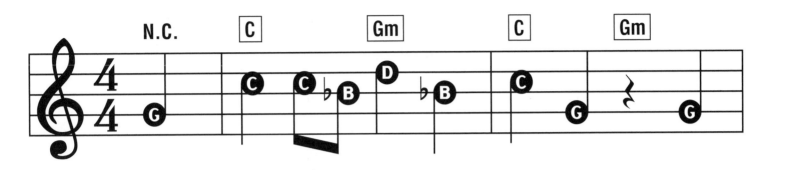

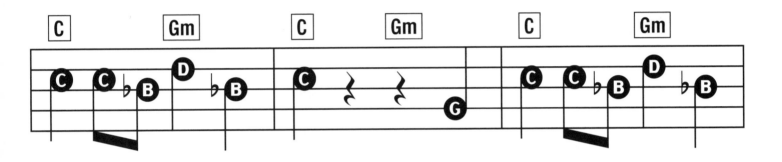

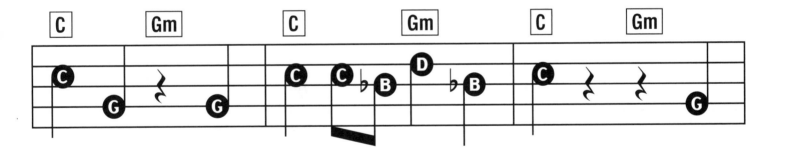

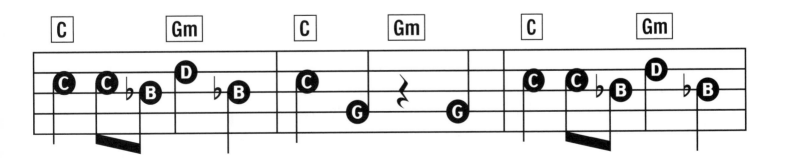

62

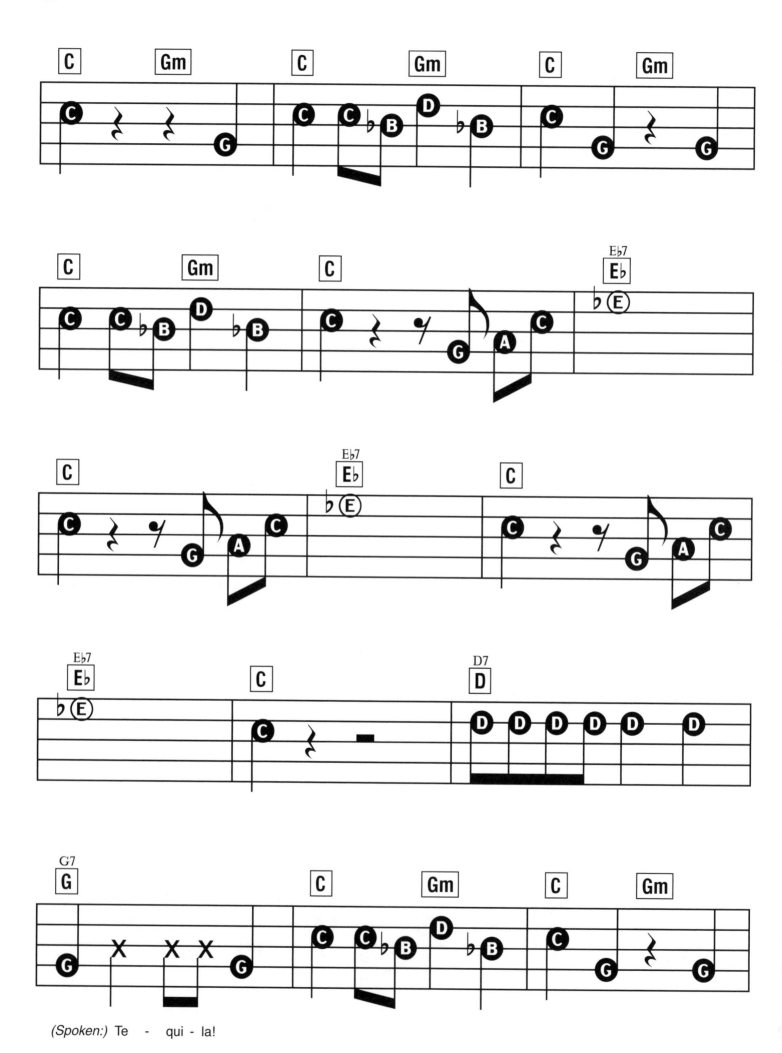

(Spoken:) Te - qui - la!

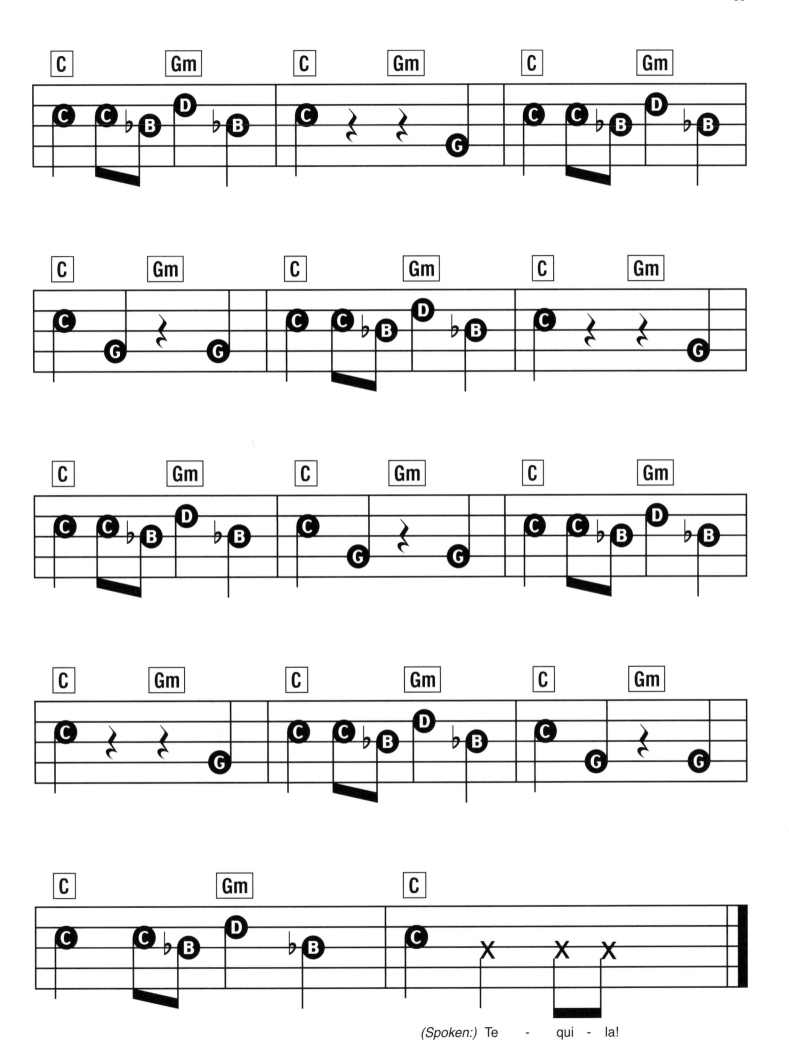

(Spoken:) Te - qui - la!

Rebel 'Rouser

Registration 4
Rhythm: Fox Trot or Country Rock

By Duane Eddy
and Lee Hazlewood

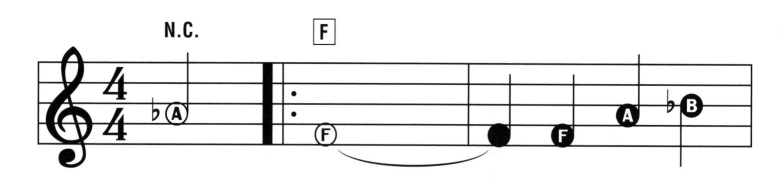

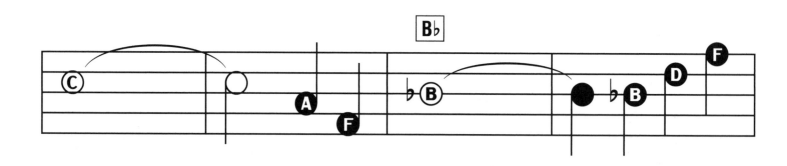

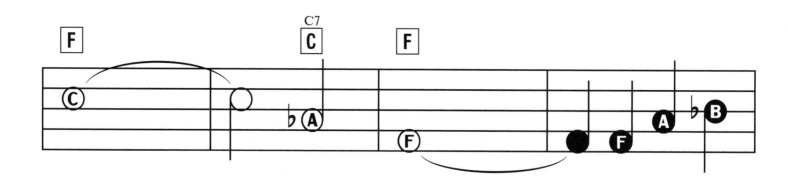

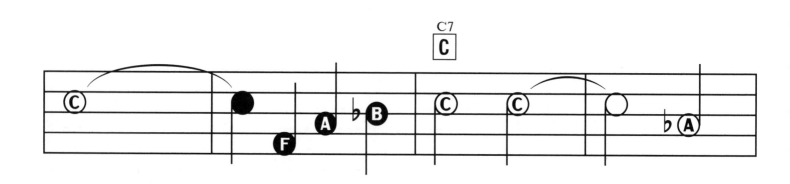

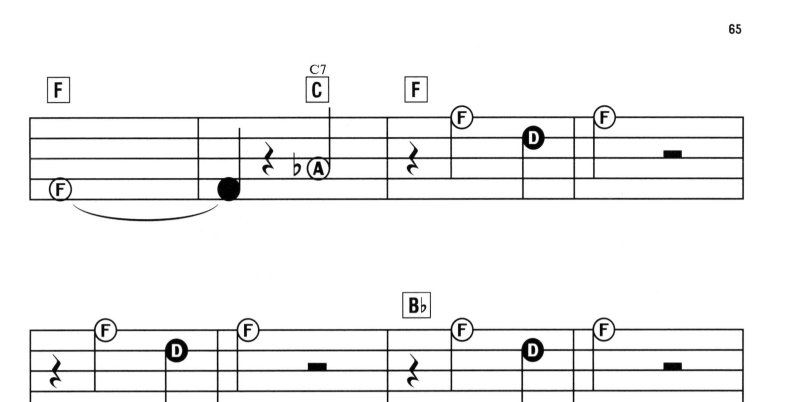

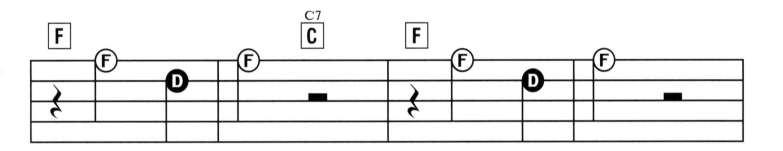

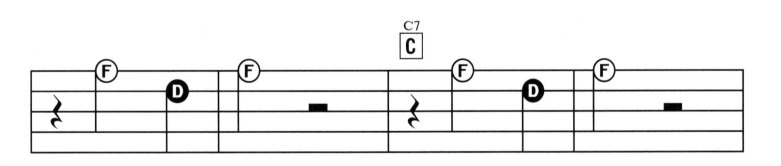

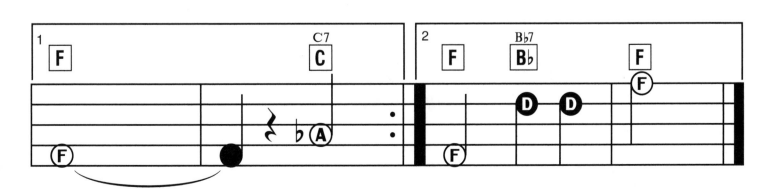

Sleepwalk

By Santo Farina,
John Farina and Ann Farina

Registration 9
Rhythm: Blues

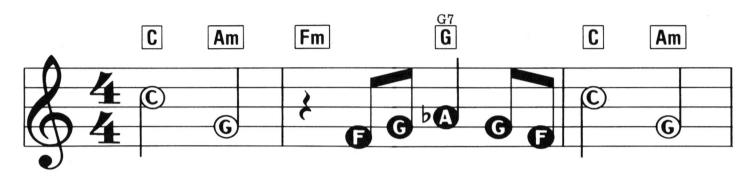

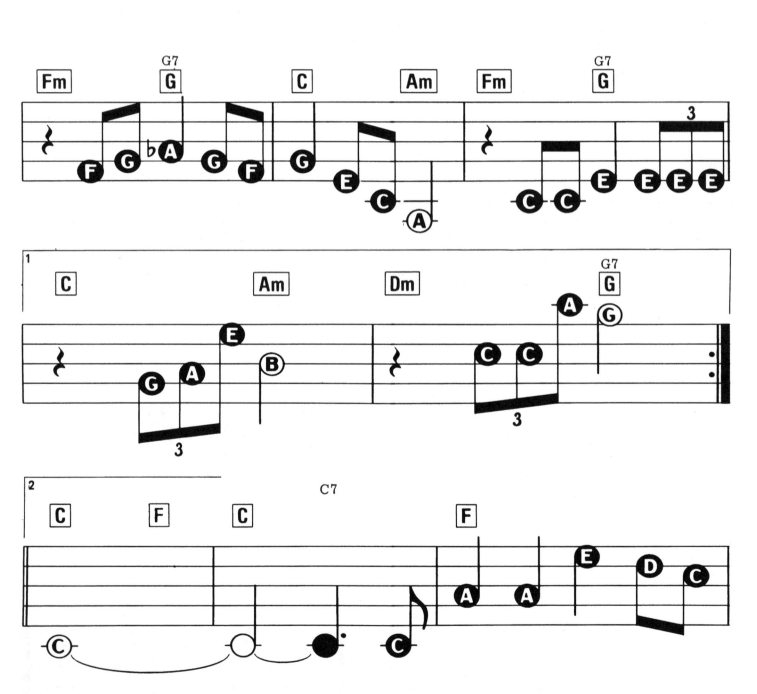

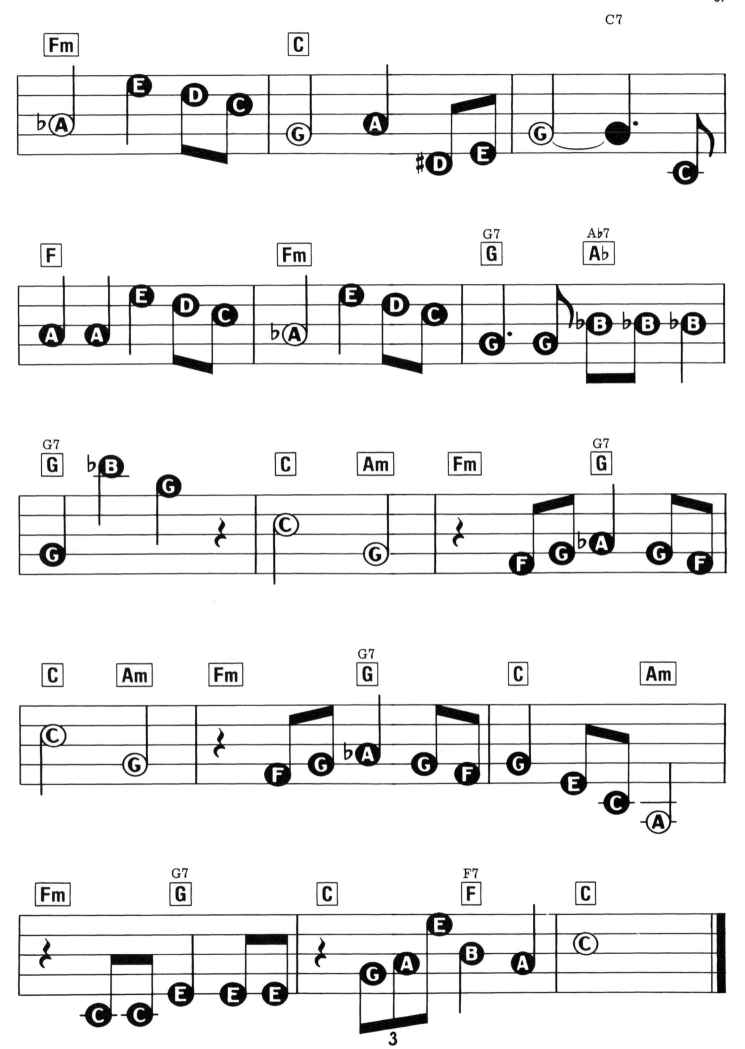

Stranger on the Shore
from FLAMINGO KID

Registration 7
Rhythm: Swing or Jazz

Words by Robert Mellin
Music by Acker Bilk

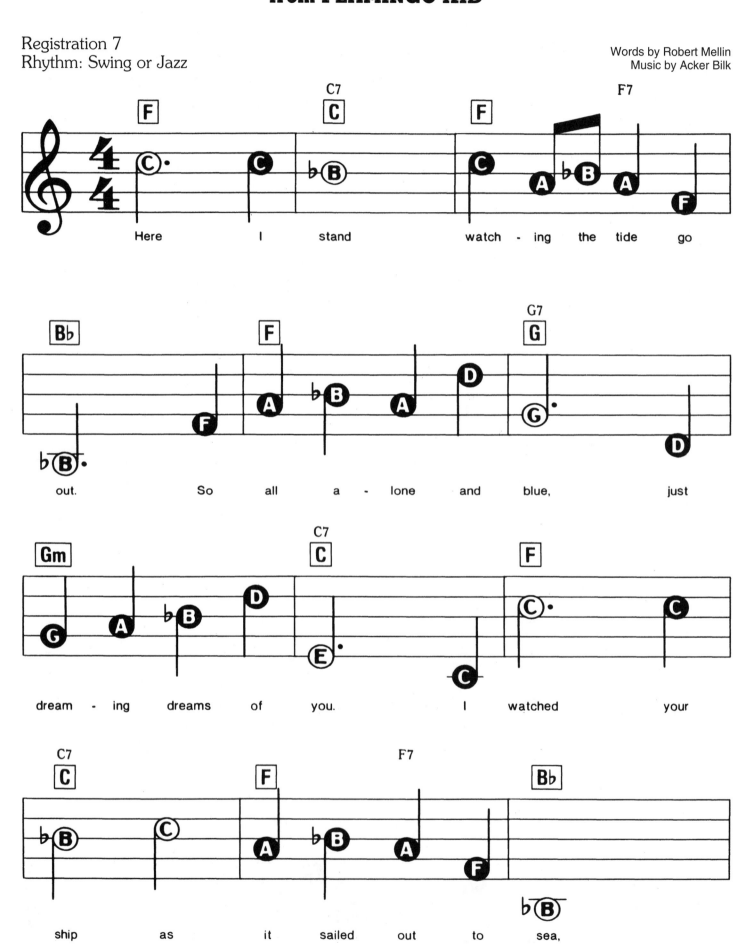

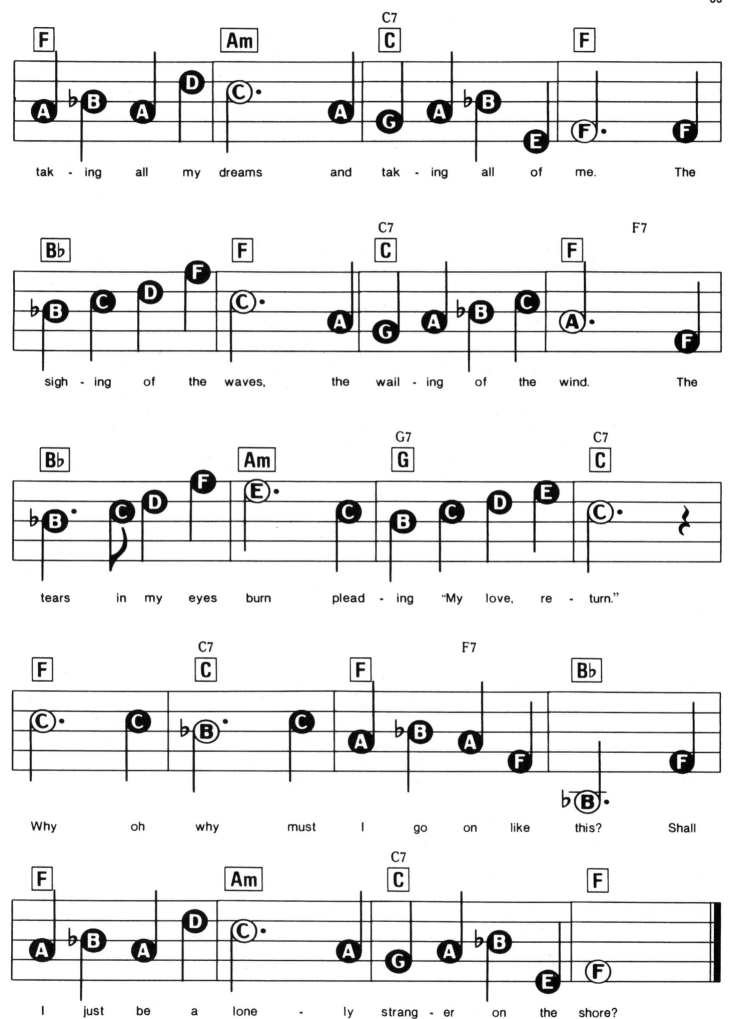

The Stripper
from THE STRIPPER

Registration 5
Rhythm: Swing or Shuffle

Music by David Rose

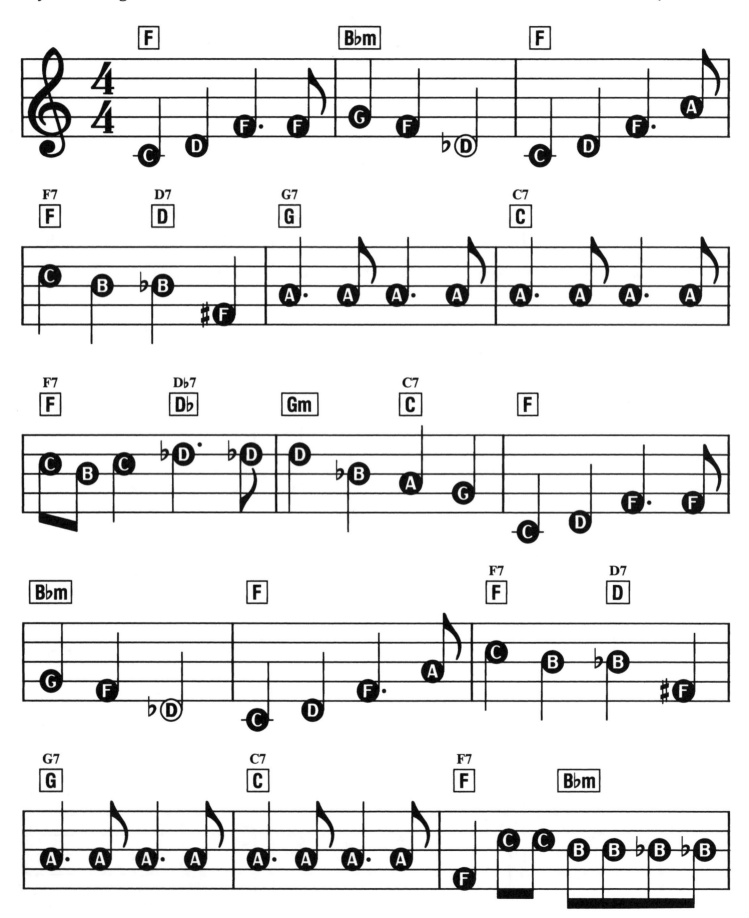

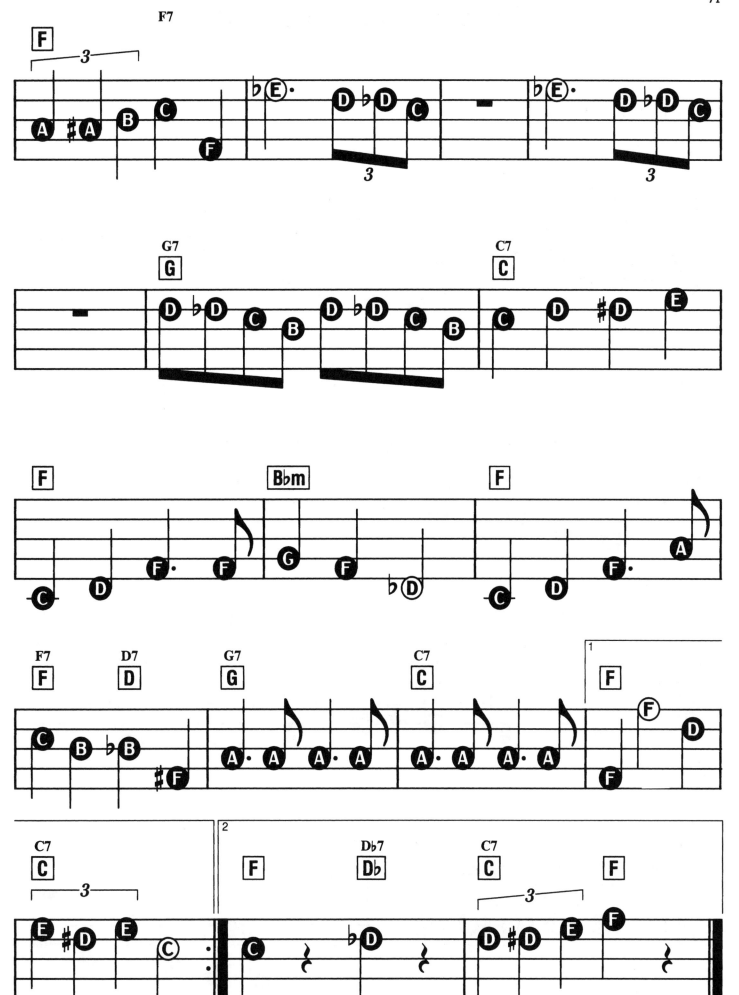

Walk Don't Run

Registration 5
Rhythm: Rock or 8-Beat

By Johnny Smith

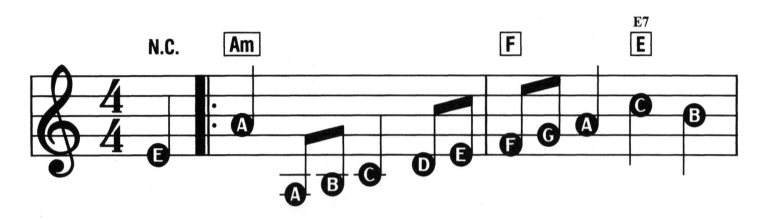

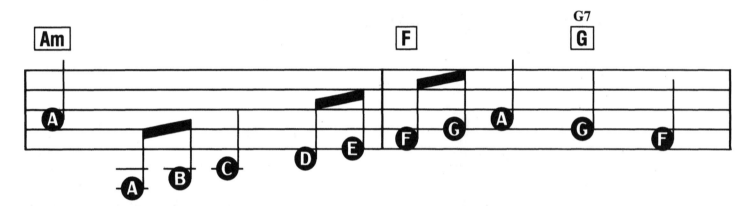

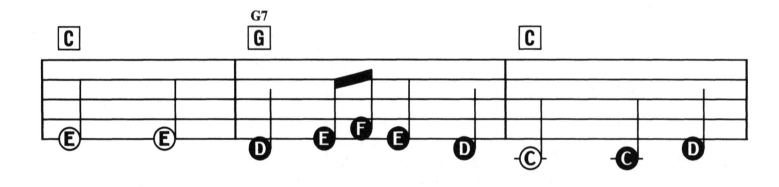

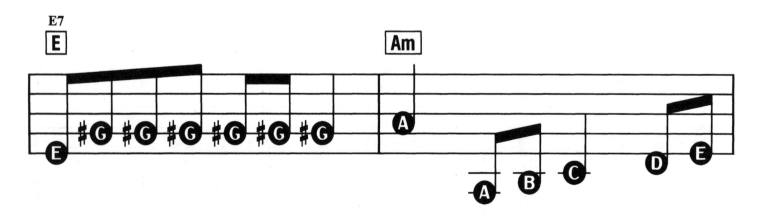

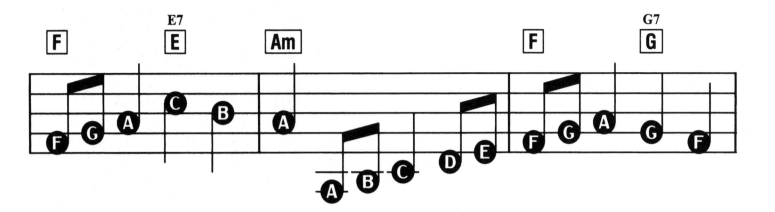

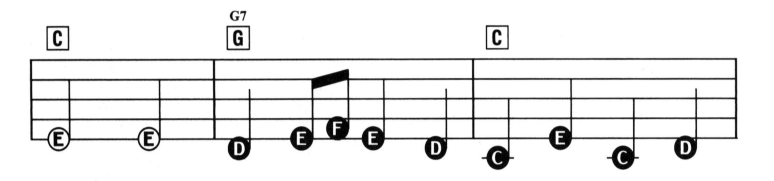

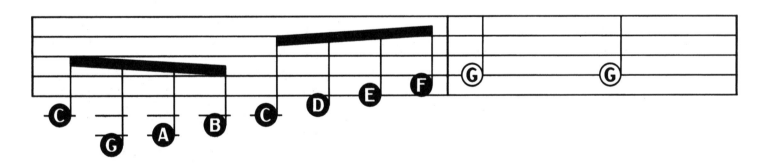

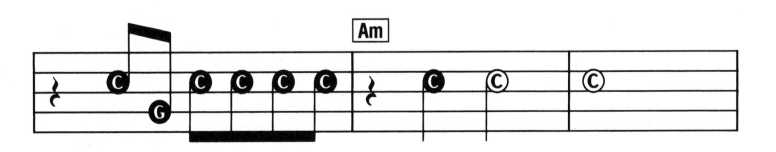

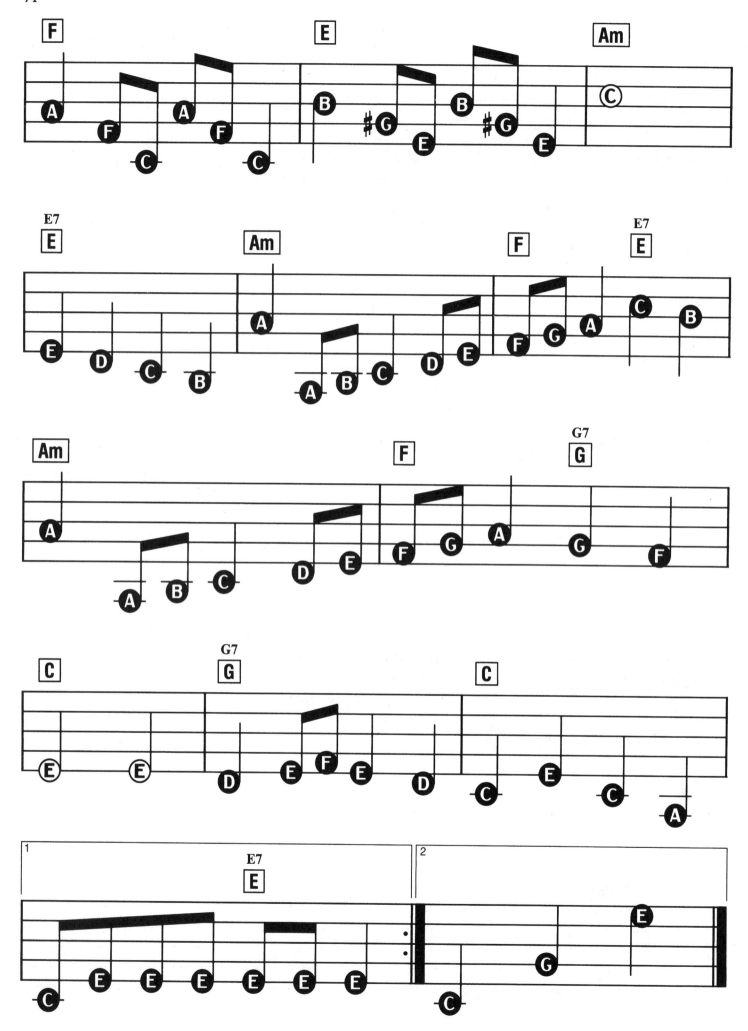

Wipe Out

Registration 4
Rhythm: Rock 'n' Roll or Rock

By The Surfaris

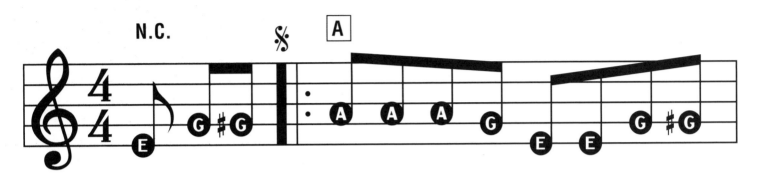

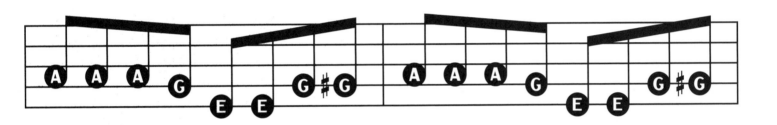

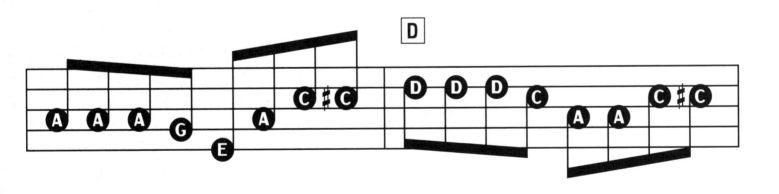

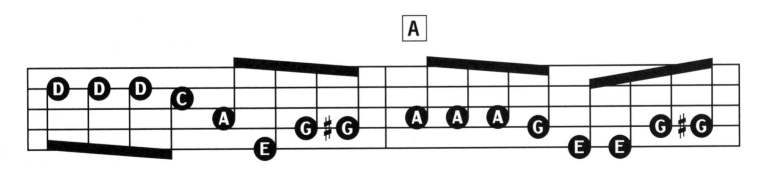

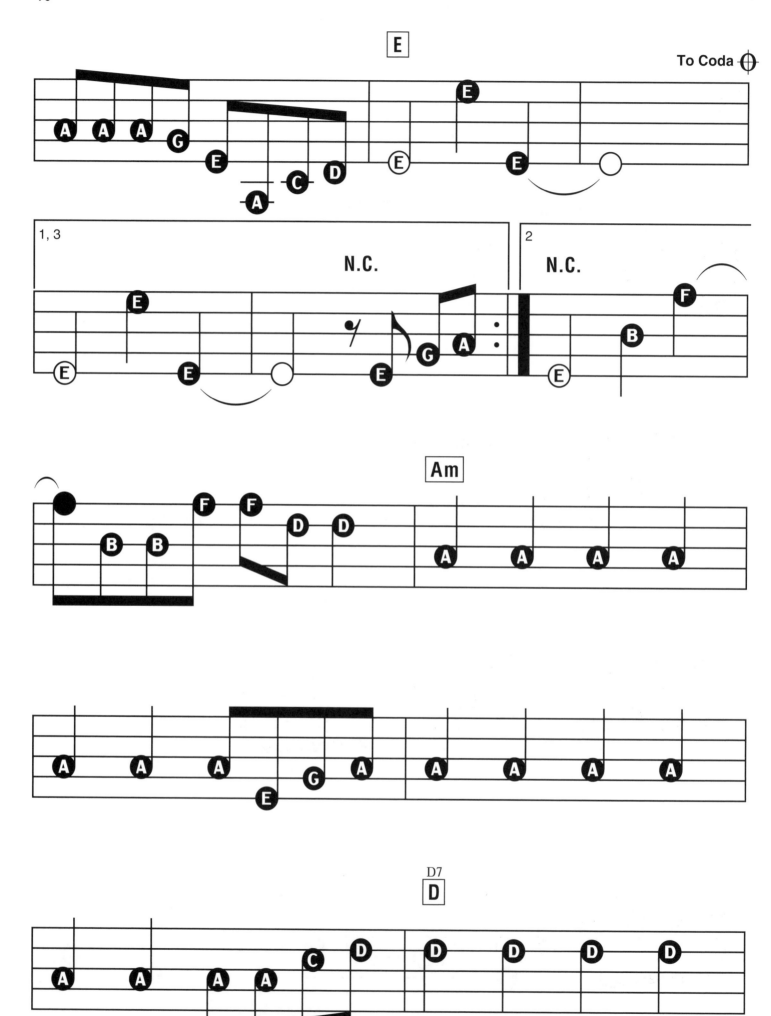

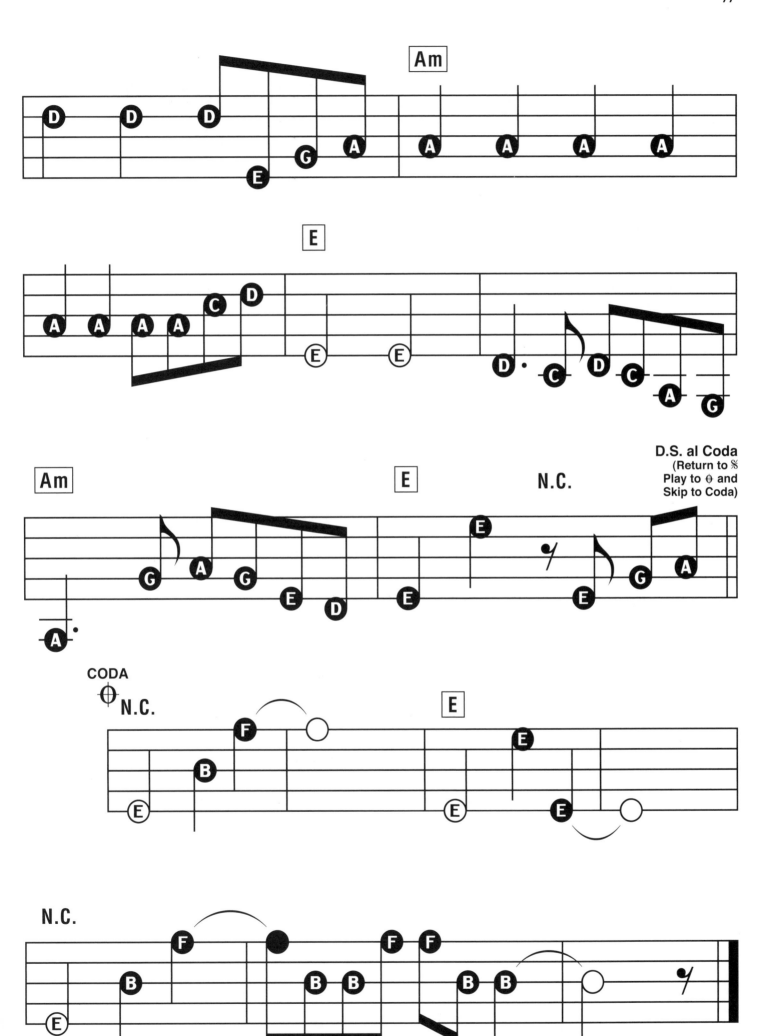

Registration Guide

- Match the Registration number on the song to the corresponding numbered category below. Select and activate an instrumental sound available on your instrument.

- Choose an automatic rhythm appropriate to the mood and style of the song. (Consult your Owner's Guide for proper operation of automatic rhythm features.)

- Adjust the tempo and volume controls to comfortable settings.

Registration

1	Mellow	Flutes, Clarinet, Oboe, Flugel Horn, Trombone, French Horn, Organ Flutes
2	Ensemble	Brass Section, Sax Section, Wind Ensemble, Full Organ, Theater Organ
3	Strings	Violin, Viola, Cello, Fiddle, String Ensemble, Pizzicato, Organ Strings
4	Guitars	Acoustic/Electric Guitars, Banjo, Mandolin, Dulcimer, Ukulele, Hawaiian Guitar
5	Mallets	Vibraphone, Marimba, Xylophone, Steel Drums, Bells, Celesta, Chimes
6	Liturgical	Pipe Organ, Hand Bells, Vocal Ensemble, Choir, Organ Flutes
7	Bright	Saxophones, Trumpet, Mute Trumpet, Synth Leads, Jazz/Gospel Organs
8	Piano	Piano, Electric Piano, Honky Tonk Piano, Harpsichord, Clavi
9	Novelty	Melodic Percussion, Wah Trumpet, Synth, Whistle, Kazoo, Perc. Organ
10	Bellows	Accordion, French Accordion, Mussette, Harmonica, Pump Organ, Bagpipes